"*Reshaping Reality* is a pra‹ that values growth, giving, and ⋯⋯⋯ a difference in the world. I'm proud of our family office's innovative leadership and proud to see its story included here. I believe we can pause to consider new possibilities. If you think that, you'll want to read it."

— **Mike Mathile**, Chairman of the Board, CYMI Holdings

"This is a must-read book for family office professionals and owners of wealth alike. *Reshaping Reality* is filled with important lessons, rich in examples, and poses provoking reflection questions."

— **Joe Astrachan**, former editor of *Family Business Review* and *Journal of Family Business Strategy*

"This fascinating book is a thoughtful resource and an impressive addition to the family office field."

— **Barbara R Hauser, JD, Ph.D.**, Founding Editor-in-Chief of the *International Family Offices Journal*, and author of *The Benefits of Applying the Rule of Law in Family Governance*

"*Reshaping Reality* offers a comprehensive look into how family offices can take underlying family business values and become a real force for good, building on their different pillars of capital and the development of individuals to make a measurable and collective impact. It is a must-read for people in the family office space."

—**Paul Andrews**, Founder, and CEO, Family Business United, The Family Business Champions

"Whether you're a family member, a single family office executive, or simply interested in understanding more about how family offices can stay relevant and effective in today's rapidly changing landscape, I highly recommend this book as a must-read."

—**Tom McCullough**, Chairman and CEO, Northwood Family Office, and co-author of *Wealth of Wisdom: The Top 50 Questions Wealthy Families Ask*

"If you have one rising generation family or affinity member who is voluntarily a client of your family office or one you represent – well done – then please read this book to know how to encourage more. If you have no such family member, *you must* read this book, and you might have one join."

—**James E. Hughes, Jr.**, author of *Family Wealth: Keeping it in the Family*

"*Reshaping Reality* explains the importance of 'putting the family's purpose, meaning, and development at its center.' It also shows family office executives how to serve as advisors and catalysts for change in the family enterprise. Finally, the authors offer strategies to build a strong partnership with the family by creating a culture of trust, commitment, accountability, and results for the family office."

—**Sara Hamilton**, Founder and Board Chair, Family Office Exchange

"*Reshaping Reality* is a breath of fresh air. It provides the reader with the information necessary to address the more complex world of single family offices today. It is both aspirational and practical."

—**Kathryn M. McCarthy**, Independent Advisor to families and family offices.

# RESHAPING REALITY

Unlocking the Potential

of the Single Family Office

Edited by Greg McCann and Jill Barber

Generation6 Innovation Series

A Generation6 Publication

Generation6.com

ISBN: 979-8-9882676-0-7

## generation6
### INNOVATION SERIES

Scan the QR code for more information about the Generation6 Innovation Series.

*To the families, the professionals who serve them,*

*and the communities they impact.*

# Acknowledgements

For an event such as the Single Family Office Gathering to come together, takes the effort, time, and talent of numerous people. It's only fitting, therefore, that we take a moment and acknowledge those good people. We would like to start by thanking the organizations that we're proud to represent for their support:

For Jill, it's CYMI and the Mathile Family for their continued support of innovation for the Family Office and growth opportunities for their employees, and Aileron, a member of the Mathile Family Enterprise and supporter of entrepreneurs and family businesses, who was a gracious host for this event.

For Greg, it's Generation6. Having two of the founders involved and having this be the first of the firm's Generation6 Innovation Series is a source of pride for Greg.

Next, we want to thank the authors. This project began as an idea, and it took a leap of faith for everyone who committed to writing a chapter. Each one of these authors is as talented as they are generous.

One of the powerful moments of this generous collaboration occurred early on in our dialog, when we co-created the list of design flaws that has become the anchor for this book.

Our heartfelt thanks to Stacy Allred, Senior Managing Director in the Financial Services Industry; Paul Carbone, Co-Founder and President of Pritzker Private Capital; James (Jim) Coutré, Vice President, Fidelity Family Offices Services; Mary Duke, Independent Advisor to Families; Andrew Keyt, Founder, and CEO, Generation6; and Jill Shipley, Managing Director, Alvarium Tiedemann | AlTi. Thanks also go to Chris Ernst, Chief Learning Officer at Workday, for contributing a foreword.

Our thanks also goes to Lisa Bennett, an author and award-winning journalist who was a consulting editor on this book. While we were the subject matter experts, Lisa was instrumental in creating a cohesive book, improving all our writing, and making our ideas more accessible.

Next, we would like to thank the people who attended this single family office gathering and gave insightful feedback to us on how to improve the book. They include Jesús Casado, Advisor, Generation6; Joni Fedders, President, Aileron; Jane Flanagan, Director of Family Office Advisory, Northern Trust Company; Christine Franco, President, Ingeborg; Buck Hinkle, Hinkle Holding Co., LLC; Kaley Hudson, Legacy Coach & Consultant, Legacy Capitals; Holly Isdale, President & CEO, Wealthaven; Timothy R. Kelly, Founder, JMC Advisors, LLC; Todd Litzsinger, Chairman, former CEO, Follett Corporation; Diane O. Malarik, President, Moreland Management Co.; Tracy Kirkland Payne, Director and Treasurer, Family Office Services, Cockrell Interests, LLC; Sarah Kerr Severson, Partner, ArentFox Schiff LLP; Tiffani Schuh, H.G. Fenton Co.; Tim Volk, Founder and Principal, T. Volk & Co.; Tom White, Chairman & CEO, Haws Corporation.

Each of these noble souls devoted time, thought, and effort into reading these chapters, traveling to Aileron in Dayton, Ohio, and sharing their thoughts. Their voice, we believe representative of our field, is artfully captured in the Voices of the Field chapter (another stellar effort by Lisa Bennett).

We want to thank and acknowledge Sara Hamilton, Founder and Board Chair, The Family Office Exchange for her thoughtful feedback.

A special thanks needs to be given to Audra Jolliffe, the project coordinator. Her tireless work at keeping everything on track, herding cats, scheduling meetings, and thinking about the million and one things we overlooked, is priceless. Thanks also to Brian Myrick, Creative Director, who not only brought his talent to creating the cover for this book, but also the layout. And, thanks to Kelly Warner and Courtney Sturgeon who assisted with all the intricate details required to gather this group together and create a space for innovation to thrive.

Finally, we'd like to extend heartfelt thanks to each other for having the courage and commitment to bring about this event and this book.

Jill Barber and Greg McCann

# Contents

# Foreword

## By Chris Ernst, Ph.D.

**Everything is, or soon will be, connected.** The most pressing challenges we face — climate change, economic inequality, global access to healthcare and education, and civic and community revitalization — are interdependent. They can only be solved by groups working collaboratively across boundaries.

We need a new way of organizing human endeavor, one more concerned with solving big challenges for all our futures rather than winning the next battle that the other group loses.

As I've gotten to know Greg McCann over the past decade, as well as Jill Barber in recent conversation, I've come to greatly respect their deep and hands-on understanding of how we navigate interdependence in our world. While we are bound together as one global society, Greg and Jill have had a transformative impact, in particular, on the essential relationships between family offices and families.

They also understand, as this book's subtitle suggests, that we all have an opportunity to make a difference.

Let me share a little about myself to explain why it would benefit you to read this book. As an advisor to leaders, my work has engaged CEOs of innovative companies in Silicon Valley to generals and ambassadors in war-torn conflicts to the founders of nonprofits both globally and locally. Out of these experiences—and both my successes and setbacks along the way—I've written extensively in leading outlets about the growing interdependence of our world, including co-authoring the best-selling book, *Boundary Spanning Leadership*.

But perhaps my most significant experience and lesson learned about the necessity of interdependent leadership was impressed upon me when I served as Director of People and Organization Potential at the Bill and Melinda Gates Foundation. As the foundation Trustees Warren Buffett, Bill Gates, and Melinda French Gates recognize, we can't envision the challenges a hundred years from now, let alone ten years out. What is important to them—and ultimately what guides the foundation's investments—is what difference we can make *right now*.

That speaks to why this book is so important. To make a difference, wealthy families and people working in single family offices must start by looking within themselves. They need to understand their values, principles, and approach to learning. And they must be exposed to different views and perspectives. This will determine the areas of focus and investment and how that translates into practice.

That's a significant shift. The traditional model was focused on finances, but the new model promises to align your finances with your purpose. It is about using the gifts we have in the time we have. That's the definition of an intentional, well-led life.

I want to acknowledge that, these days, many of us have times when we feel overwhelmed and even hopeless about the many challenging issues of our day. But take heart!

This book shows that every family can make choices that are aligned with their deeper purpose in the company of other families aligning with their deeper purpose. And as those pieces come together, we can transform communities and the fabric of society as a whole.

That is the great promise of this book.

# Introduction

## By Greg McCann and Jill Barber

**Over the past twenty years,** I (Greg McCann) have specialized in working with family enterprises on leadership development, communication and conflict resolution, transitions, and helping the next generation succeed in their careers and lives.

During this time, I felt that although I was traveling from city to city and town to town, I was encountering the same dynamic. There was widespread frustration and wasted energy—as if very competent professionals were stuck in an overly narrow conception of their abilities and mission.

In short, there was untapped potential. And I knew more could be accomplished—with the right vision, strategy, and people willing to pioneer this work. Then I began working with Jill Barber, my co-editor on this book and President of CYMI Holdings, a single family office in Dayton, Ohio.

Jill grew up in an entrepreneurial home. Her dad was a farmer and the owner of a construction company. She watched and learned from him. Then she went to college and became a tax manager for Arthur Andersen. Finally, in 1999, she joined CYMI Holdings, rising from Assistant Controller to Chief Client Service Officer and President. It was this last role for which she felt both prepared and unprepared.

It's true! Like most people in my industry, I (Jill Barber) was hired for my subject matter expertise. But I soon learned that subject matter expertise had yet to prepare me to be a truly successful family office leader in these changing times.

In January 2020, Greg visited our offices to meet with our management team. I'd already been consulting with him as my coach for about six months. So, it surprised me when several people on my team told Greg they felt they weren't being heard by the rest of the leadership team or me. They asked him to facilitate a conversation with me and other members of our leadership team.

That was my "ah-hah" moment. Until then, I had been trying to make changes on my own, and it wasn't working. There was dysfunction, distrust, misunderstanding, and frustration all around. Finally, I realized that if I were going to become the leader I wanted to be—and help our family office achieve its potential in partnership with our family—we would all need to learn new skills.

Over the next year, under Greg's guidance, I worked with my leadership team on developing trust-based leadership and team building based on a three-tiered model of the role of leadership. This is a vertical leadership development model where we focused on three levels of leadership.

The first level in this model is the Expert. At this stage, our mindset is that we must always be busy doing. We tend to frame things as problems the leader should solve and we see the leader as connecting with each team member individually. We think of ourselves as the spoke and the team as the wheel. The second level is the Achiever. Here, leaders can still do problem-solving but now have the capacity to focus more on strategic outcomes and a systems perspective. We are also more mindful of gaining buy-in and coordinating efforts with team members. Finally, the third or higher, is the Catalyst. At this level, a leader (who also still retains the capacity for problem-solving and systems thinking) also has the added capacity of being a visionary who focuses less on themselves and more on the team. (See our chapter for a fuller discussion and related citation.)

Of course, as you evolve to higher levels, you still retain the capacity of the former level. The point is to develop an agile leadership style that lets you know how and when to switch between the capacities. For example, my team may need me to just solve a problem, such as "The building is on fire. Get everyone out!" Other times the team may need me to take a step back from an immediate problem (such as Ralph wanting a raise) and see the system (in this case, the equity of our compensation packages.) And other times, my ideal role is to be a catalyst who can envision how we can maximize our potential or shape our culture to serve the interests of our family.

There was much more to what my team and I learned while working with Greg—and the outcomes were transformative. But the bottom line is this work showed that there is so much more potential for what family offices and families can achieve—if we were willing to grow beyond being limited to subject matter experts alone.

I also discovered, as Greg had before me, that unlocking the true potential of the family office begins with recognizing the design flaws inherent in the relationship between the family office and the families we serve—then envisioning a new way of working together.

To put it another way, we saw the time is ripe for the next evolution of the family office. And that is what we hope to inspire a conversation about with this book.

*Reshaping Reality: Unlocking the Potential of the Family Office* is a collection of essays written by leading thinkers in this field, Stacy Allred, Paul Carbone, Jim Coutré, Mary Duke, Andrew Keyt, Jill Shipley, and the two of us.

Our goal is to dive into the challenge encapsulated by an adage we hear from many people working in family offices today: You have one client (the family) who is also your boss, who doesn't understand the field and doesn't want to—which results in the family outsourcing the responsibility or ownership of the single family office.

We met virtually for a year to discuss this project and share ideas and chapter drafts. Then we gathered at the offices of Aileron, a leadership institute in Dayton, Ohio, to present the chapters to a circle of guests who represented the field. They included family members, family office executives, and advisors. We asked for their critique and then edited the chapters accordingly, hoping to distill only the best ideas to share with you, the readers of this book.

So, what will you find here?

First, we identify ten design flaws or challenges inherent in the single family office. These range from many family offices having a paradoxical attitude toward wealth to an absence of agility that these fast-changing times demand for family enterprises to remain successful.

Jill Shipley, Managing Director, Alvarium Tiedemann | AlTi, sets the stage with a chapter on how wealth perception shapes reality. Paul Carbone, Co-Founder and President of Pritzker Private Capital, writes about the Antidote to Private Equity. Jim Coutré, Vice President, Insights and Connections at Fidelity Family Office Services, writes about family office relevancy: doing what's asked and what's needed. Mary Duke, an internationally recognized advisor to families navigating the complexities of substantial wealth, and Stacy Allred, Senior Managing Director and Head of Family Engagement and Governance with a financial firm, write about the role of learning in the family-centered office. Andrew Keyt, Founder and CEO of Generation6 and an internationally known business strategist and succession planning expert, addresses the transformative family office. And we (Greg and Jill), address family office leadership—through a genuine case study on leadership development and teamwork.

We hope that this book deepens the conversation about what can be achieved in single family offices, allows you to step back and find a fresh way to work *on* the family office and not just in it, and ultimately helps you place humans, not just money, at the center of your work. And while there should be no prescribed path for every family and family office, we hope it offers some concrete ideas for improving your important work.

Finally, we hope this book convinces you that if you are thinking about the family office and how to make it have a greater impact, you are not alone. You have a tribe!

# Design Flaws or the Places We Can Innovate From

"Design is not just what it looks like and feels like.
Design is how it works."

—Steve Jobs

It's a bit unconventional—in fact, it might seem downright silly—to name this chapter "Design Flaws" and then immediately establish some conditions on what we mean by that phrase. But a driving goal of this book is to inspire bold, out-of-the-box thinking about what comes next for single family offices. And that requires that we begin with a bit of a tough love perspective on the conditions that might be holding us back. Then, we can better imagine, as children's book author Dr. Seuss might have said, the places we can go—or, as we would more tamely put it: how we can unlock the potential of the single family office.

So, let's begin with an understanding of what is usually meant by "design flaws." According to Cornell Law School, a design flaw (or, more specifically, in their terminology, a design defect) is inherent in the design rather than the production of a product that results in something dangerous to consumers.

One recent example is the recall of one million Teslas. The company recognized a design flaw in their windows, which caused them to close even if someone's arm was resting on them. Because computers control them, the fix was easy. Tesla owners weren't required to bring their cars in. Instead, the design was corrected remotely, causing the incident to be dubbed "the recall that wasn't."

A more famous—and disastrous—design flaw example is the Ford Pinto. Ford produced this car from 1971 to 1976, when a massive recall and scandal shut down production. The problem? Pintos could easily catch fire and explode because there was a lack of reinforcement between the fuel tank and the rear bolts. So, if you owned a Ford Pinto and another car rolled into your back bumper—even at a speed as slow as 20 m.p.h.—boom! You could be in serious trouble.

In both cases and countless others, the problem did not rest with the people who were making the cars. Instead, they inherited an issue that came before they got to work. It was inherent in the design of their work.

So, how does this apply to single family offices? We are fortunately not in the business of producing products that can cause physical injury and death! But we have inherited certain conditions that we operate under that can prevent us from doing our best work—especially in today's fast-changing world.

We should hasten to add this idea is not unique to single family offices. For example, a 2019 article in *The Harvard Business Review* identified at least four organizational design issues that most leaders

misdiagnose. Ron Carucci, co-founder and Managing Partner at Navalent, an organizational and leadership development consultancy firm, identified these as poor governance, bad role design, excessive spans of control, and misaligned incentives or metrics.[1]

In the case of single family offices, we have identified ten design flaws—or, more neutrally, issues that we find inherently challenging or limiting. These range from the very nature of family relationships to expectations that suggest single family office staff must do *everything* for families. We offer them here for your consideration of how they may apply in your single family office—and as a roadmap for the following chapters, as each address one or more of the design flaws identified here.

As you reflect on them, we encourage you to remember—that much like the makers of the Ford Pinto—single family office staff and, for the large part, today's families are not responsible for these flaws. Instead, they are the conditions we have come to work under that we now have an opportunity to reconsider as we seek to unlock the potential of the single family office.

## Top 10 Design Flaws of the Single Family Office (SFO)

1. **Family relationships are inherently complex—and infinitely more so when wealth is involved.**

   - Family wealth creates artificial entanglements between people who might not otherwise be in a relationship with each other.

---

[1] Harvard Business Review. "4 Organizational Design Issues That Most Leaders Misdiagnose," December 16, 2019. https://hbr.org/2019/12/4-organizational-design-issues-that-most-leaders-misdiagnose.

- These trust structures tie people and their choices together in ways that can foster animosity when people have differing values, social agendas, levels of risk tolerance, and so on.

- The artificial entanglements created by family wealth create obstacles to flourishing that cannot be overcome without conscious effort.

- Many of the complexities are unexamined, which leads to a lack of understanding.

2. **Many families and the SFOs that serve them lack a unifying sense of purpose.**

- Related to lacking a sense of purpose, families often fail to take emotional ownership for their family office.

- Many family members who have inherited their wealth feel a disconnect between what their money is invested in and what matters to them. They also feel uncertain about how to create more alignment.

- There is a widespread failure to break through the old Andrew Carnegie mindset that the best thing to do is make wealth at any cost and then try to do a little good with some of it.

- There is a lack of incentives and processes for aligning wealth with the best interests of the individual, family, and society.

- There is also often a lack of desire to work through varying views of family members to achieve a unifying purpose, with some seeing the raising of differences as a personal attack or judgments best avoided altogether.

3. A lack of purpose leads to lost opportunities.

- Families lose the opportunity to direct their wealth, at least partly, to a purpose beyond its maintenance and growth.

- Society loses the benefits that could come from wealth being more directly aligned with activities that foster the greater good.

- The professional staff in family offices lose the opportunity to connect with the family around a greater sense of purpose.

4. Many SFOs have a paradoxical attitude toward family wealth.

- On the one hand, they see it as the be-all-and-end-all asset they must preserve and grow for the family.

- On the other hand, they recognize that inherited wealth can negatively affect family members and feel they have to protect them.

5. SFOs are based on what would, in any other domain, be seen as an untenable business model: a single client.

- The single client is also their boss.

- The majority of family members also lack an understanding of the industry—and any intention to understand it.

- The only way to grow clients is for members of the existing

xxiv    **Reshaping Reality**

client to have more children!

6. **There is a widespread lack of understanding between families and family offices.**

- Few families are interested in overseeing the work of the family office—that is, stepping into the role of an active owner.

- Some family members also lack the knowledge of how to be owners and prioritize family relationships over SFO leadership—leaving a leadership vacuum, especially when conflicts arise.

- Family office staff often have fixed, narrow views about family members.

- There is a lack of accountability between families and family offices and the processes and incentives that would establish this.

7. **There is too little diversity of thought.**

- By nature, a single family tends to have less diversity of thought than a group of individuals from different backgrounds.

- Often, the family office staff are in risk-averse professions.

- This increases the need for a diverse team of advisors to ensure the long-term success of the family enterprise.

- This lack of diversity undermines innovation.

8. **There is an absence of agility that these fast-changing times**

demand for family enterprises to remain successful.

- Agility can be developed through coaching and other professional development opportunities. But there is little professional development happening in families and SFOs. This flows partly from family offices being seen as a cost center, not as an investment.

9.  **SFOs are primarily staffed by technical specialists.**

    - This perpetuates the undermining of a deeper sense of purpose.

    - It also leads to an unnecessarily myopic focus on technical work that could be outsourced, undermining the SFO's reason for being.

    - Lacking background and professional development in visionary leadership, emotional intelligence, and other people skills, many SFOs lean toward easily quantifiable activities and overlook qualitative measures of success.

10. **Lacking a clear sense of purpose, many SFOs think they must do everything for the family. This creates:**

    - Unhealthy relationships based on a lack of clear boundaries and responsibilities.

    - Dependency by family members on the SFO for things the family should be dealing with—such as advice about marital disputes.

    - An unclear sense of their value.

CHAPTER

# Wealth: Perception Shapes Reality

## By Jill Shipley

**Let's start with a quick activity.** Take two minutes and write down all the words that come to mind when you think of "wealth" or "wealthy." Write down whatever arises. Once you have a list of at least five words, consider whether the word is positive, negative, neutral, or both. Did you think something like "hard-working" or "entitled?" Consider why these words came to mind. Is this a perspective you heard or learned about wealth growing up? Is the word a connotation that society or the media link to wealth? Reflect on your attitudes, biases, and perceptions about wealth and the wealthy, and consider where these opinions came from. Here is a list of the most common answers I have heard.

| POSITIVE | NEGATIVE |
|---|---|
| Success | Greedy |
| Hard work | Burden |
| Freedom | Guilt |
| Luxury | Unfair |
| Fun | Gluttony |
| Security | Snob |
| Intelligent | Entitled |
| Entrepreneurial | Selfish |

For the last twenty years, I have asked this question to ultra-wealthy families, the top one percent in society.

Consider how the words that immediately arose in your mind compare with my experience with wealth creators and inheritors and the research on wealth stereotypes described below.

Wealth creators tend to provide mostly positive comments such as freedom, hard work, and success. Wealth creators may express words like "luck" or "responsibility," some citing it as positive, some neutral, or negative. Words such as "greed" or "entitled" are negative examples referencing the stereotype of wealthy people. Clients often express a caveat reflecting on themselves, saying, "We try hard not to act that way," "We are raising our kids to be grounded," or even "We are not wealthy."

A UBS study found that 40 percent of individuals with $5 million in investable assets did not define themselves as wealthy.[2]

Inheritors (especially generation X, Y, and Z) typically share more negative responses than positive ones. They share words such as "burden," "inequitable," "guilt," or "waste." Inheritors also often express that wealth comes with a lot of responsibility which can be both positive and challenging. They say that wealth opens doors and provides more significant opportunities and options, which they describe as both a blessing and a difficulty that can be paralyzing.

---

[2]UBS Wealth Management Americas' fourth UBS Investor Watch, 2013.

[3]Pew Research Study, https://www.pewresearch.org/fact-tank/2021/07/28/americans-views-about-billionaires-have-grown-somewhat-more-negative-since-2020/.

The other 99 percent of the population also share positive and negative attitudes about wealth. A Pew Research Study asking how the rich are different from the average American, found the rich to be perceived as more intelligent and hard-working, but also more greedy and dishonest.[3]

Rainer Zitelmann's 2020 book, *The Rich in Public Opinion: What We Think When We Think About Wealth*, examines attitudes about wealth in Germany, the United States, France, and Great Britain. He notes the wealthy are seemingly the one minority group that is discriminated against, even hated, with no backlash or criticism. Zitelmann finds people generally admire the wealthy but also envy them, sometimes at a toxic level. When asked about perceptions of millionaires, the most frequently mentioned traits across these Western nations include positive characteristics, such as intelligence, boldness, daring, and visionary. Negative attributes include self-centeredness, materialism, ruthlessness, and greediness.[4]

While there are positive and negative stereotypes of wealth and the wealthy, negative prejudices and stereotypes are more common and pernicious than positive ones.

Why does all of this matter? The most straightforward answer is that when negative perceptions of wealth grow along with wealth inequality, this rarely leads to a positive long-term result and can contribute to unhappiness, social unrest, adverse economic effects, and political challenges.

---

[4]Zitelmann, Rainer. (2020). Upward classism: Prejudice and stereotyping against the wealthy. Economic Affairs. 40. 162-179. 10.1111/ecaf.12407.

But today, we have an opportunity to design and achieve a better result by focusing on positive perceptions of wealth; and younger generations are already expecting it of us. They expect their family's wealth to do more than grow. They expect it also to create value in the world. And many of them expect their advisors and family offices to help them achieve success based on a broader approach to capital which encompasses human, intellectual, social, spiritual, and financial capital.

This chapter establishes the context for this challenge and opportunity by discussing how wealth is commonly perceived, where those perceptions come from, and how we might redefine "wealth" and "returns" going forward.

## Where Our Biases about Wealth Come From

Before the internet, people compared their financial status to that of their neighbors. Great wealth was rarely seen in person. You heard of dynastic families like the Rockefellers and Waltons and read about or watched a movie or TV show about the life of the rich and famous. But most people did not measure their financial well-being based on these moguls. Keeping up with the Joneses was based on proximity.

Today, in contrast, we have access to social media, streaming services, and constant global connectivity in our pockets. Social media depicts what people want others to see about their lives, not their actual lives. The wealthiest individuals often have the most followers and have images or videos of their extravagant lives go viral, envied by millions. Television shows and movies accessible 24/7 focused on the lives of the rich. Huge homes, fancy cars, luxurious vacations, and endless material possessions are displayed. Life appears picture-perfect, with anything you wish for at your fingertips.

Instead of comparing our finances with our neighbors, we constantly see highly curated reminders that we have far fewer resources than others, leaving us longing for more. Although many dream of having great financial wealth, it can be hard to watch others succeed and live a dream lifestyle. Theodore Roosevelt's quote, "Comparison is the thief of joy," is confirmed in a recent Yale study that found a crucial factor in well-being is our perception of wealth and status relative to others.[5]

Here are some of our biases and how our perceptions of them can affect us.

## Security and Freedom

The dictionary defines wealth as "an abundance of valuable material possessions or resources."[6] An abundance of resources removes stressors around having enough for basic human needs such as shelter, food, and healthcare. Having your needs met brings positive associations such as security and safety. Having more financial resources than you need brings additional freedom to spend your time as you desire, to follow a passion versus work at a job you don't enjoy just to pay the bills, and to travel and relax.

---

[5]Tan, J. J. X., Kraus, M. W., Carpenter, N. C., & Adler, N. E. (2020). The association between objective and subjective socioeconomic status and subjective well-being: A meta-analytic review. Psychological Bulletin, 146 (11)

[6]Merriam-Webster Dictionary

## Respect, Hard Work, and Admiration

Building something from nothing typically takes ingenuity, dedication, sacrifice, and hard work.

The concept of the American Dream was coined in 1931 by the writer and historian James Truslow Adams. He said, "Life should be better and richer and fuller for everyone, with opportunity for each according to ability or achievement," regardless of social class or circumstances of birth.[7] Americans express admiration and respect for the immigrant story, starting with nothing and reaching ultimate success by building financial wealth.

## The Inequity of Opportunity

Negativity is enhanced if you struggle or feel others have an unfair advantage. America's origin story is grounded in inequities. White males had the right to vote, own property, make a living, and launch businesses. White males had the opportunity to grow resources and pass those resources on to their children and grandchildren. In contrast, women, Blacks, and other racial minorities did not. This racial and gender discrimination throughout our history still impacts society today. It is understandable there would be negativity toward business owners that make exponentially more than their employees, especially if the business founder inherited the business or the money to start the enterprise.

Being born into wealth is at the epicenter of inequity and nega-

---

[7]Thomas, D. Y. (1932). The Epic of America. By James Truslow Adams. (Boston: Little, Brown, and Company, 1931.)

tivity. Wealth creators tend to have positive intentions, passing wealth down and striving to give their children, grandchildren, and future generations a better life. It can feel unfair to the rest of society that individuals who did nothing to earn what they are given have a leg up. They do not have to be hard working to have their needs or wants to be met. They are typically perceived as spoiled or entitled, many being degraded as trust fund babies. It is difficult for inheritors to engender respect, including a sense of credibility, even when they create their financial success with people saying, "They think they hit a home run, but they started on third base."

Once you have acquired financial resources, you have greater access to building more wealth than the rest of society. You can access the best education, healthcare, food, and advice. It can feel unfair or unjust that wealthy individuals skip the line at a theme park, hire defense if in legal trouble or to fight a speeding ticket, or use connections to get a family member a job opportunity. The wealthy can invest as accredited investors, giving access to investment options not accessible to anyone with less than $1 million net worth. The wealthy have access to tax loopholes and tax breaks, with the average billionaire paying 8 percent tax while the average American pays 13.29 percent.[8]

## Influence of Media

The media sensationalize and reinforce the portrayal of the wealthy as

---

[8]Zitelmann, R. (2020a). The Rich in Public Opinion: What We Think, When We Think about Wealth. Washington, DC: Cato Institute.

[9]Konish, Lorie. "The Number of Billionaires Soared during the Pandemic. How Tax Proposals Aim to Reduce Wealth Inequality." CNBC, May 23, 2022. https://www.cnbc.com/2022/05/23/as-number-of-billionaires-climbs-new-calls-for-wealth-taxes-emerge.html

greedy, stingy, snobby, and wasteful. A study of over 500 films depicted rich characters as competent and daring, but their personalities are shown to be arrogant, unsympathetic, callous, immoral, and selfish.[9] Examples of greed and power can be found in movies, such as *The Wolf of Wall Street, Ocean's Thirteen,* and *Pretty Woman,* to name a few.

Wealthy families and family businesses are portrayed as corrupt, greedy, depraved, and wrought with family conflict and infighting on television series such as *Succession, Billions, Yellowstone,* and the *Sopranos.*

The negative biases attached to inheritors are reinforced in movies and TV, such as *The Ultimate Gift, Paris in Love,* and *Knives Out.*

## What it Feels Like to be a Wealth Creator

Over 80 percent of wealth holders are first-generation wealth creators, the vast majority citing they came from lower to middle-class upbringings.[10] Looking at American history, the majority of the population that arrived in North America were immigrants with limited resources. Many worked hard, determined to provide their families with a better life.

A client in his seventies shared a story of the day he was confident he would be financially successful. He was living with a friend paying for college by working two jobs and eating his daily meal of crackers he stole from a local gas station. He recalled saying to his friend, "I will never let my children live like this." He built an incredibly successful business with this roommate that they sold 30 years later for hundreds of

---

[10]Stanley, T. J., & Danko, W. D. (2010). The millionaire next door: The surprising secrets of America's wealthy (1st Taylor Trade Pub. ed.)

millions. Growing up in scarcity, he was always worried about running out to the point that his children were frustrated and embarrassed by his "cheapness."

Like many business founders, he poured his blood, sweat, and tears into the business, sacrificing significantly along the way. After the company sold, he was lost. What now? He had time and all the resources to buy all the material things imaginable. He thought if only he had the means to afford a "fancy life"—a bigger home or boat—then he would be happy. Sadly, he and many other wealth creators find themselves immigrants in this new land of wealth, concerned about being perceived as the negative stereotypes described.[11]

Imagine you are a wealth creator, similar to my client, and you worry and fear: What if money makes your children and grandchildren spoiled, entitled, or lazy. How will they understand the value of a dollar or hard work?

You may feel the need to protect yourself, your money, and your family. You may decide to move to a nicer neighborhood, send your children to get a better education at a private school, travel to more luxurious destinations for vacations, and join a country club. You become surrounded by others who have financial resources, often more disconnected from your old life and a sense of what it means to have enough.

Given time is the one thing money cannot buy, you hire people to

---

[11]Strangers in Paradise: How Families Adapt to Wealth Across Generations. by Grubman Ph.D., James (Family Wealth Consulting 2013)

help with tasks that do not bring you joy. It is convenient to delegate tasks, and there is truth to the fact you are providing others with job opportunities and income. The challenge arises when some things cannot or should not be delegated. For example, you cannot outsource building trust, showing love, and effectively communicating in a family system. Strong relationships cannot be paid for. This is not to suggest families should not hire help such as caregivers, educators, therapists, and advisors such as family office staff. Reflect on what you are gaining and what you may be giving up. An example could include using influence to get a child out of a speeding ticket or bank fee versus the child learning a lesson.

Yet after the sale of the business, the family, usually led by the wealth creator, tends not to bring the same mindset, dedication, and sense of ownership to starting the family office. In a nutshell: What it took to build wealth is not what it takes to keep it.

| Perspective and Actions of a Family Leader(s) - Business | Perspective and Actions of a Family Leader(s) - Single Family Office |
|---|---|
| Gain expertise. | Hire expertise, which may fail to develop it in the family. |
| Take ownership. | Outsource ownership. |
| Work on and in business. | May struggle to do both or lack desire for either. |
| Be clear on the purpose of the effort. | Purpose may be more defined by default. |
| Be hungry/driven/ motivated /passionate. | Often little passion or even interest in it exist. |
| Feel proud when building it and guilty when selling it. | Struggle with a new identity, career, and sense of contribution. |

| | |
|---|---|
| Use outside board to challenge. | Use of outside board to validate. |
| Network. | Isolate. |
| Push the envelope. | Maintain status quo. |
| Step back when losing interest | Become complacent. |
| Be proactive. | Become reactive. |
| Empower the family. | Enable the family. |

## What it Feels Like to be an Inheritor

Inheritors often struggle in the shadow of their family's financial success. They recognize they are different from others, but it is confusing and not typically discussed at home. Inheritors struggle to trust the authenticity of relationships, and many spend their life hiding the fact they have financial resources from friends, colleagues, and significant others. Many are embarrassed and feel guilt or shame for having more than others.

Why does everyone look to you to pay the bill at the end of a meal? Are people befriending you to sell you something or get something from you? What do you say to friends or family when they ask for financial help when you have the means to help? It is painful and difficult to watch friends struggle with debt or require a fiancé to sign a prenup, which can be perceived as planning for a divorce before marriage.

---

[12]The NonProfit Times. "Millennials Value Everyday Social Good Above Cash Donations," May 6, 2021. https://www.thenonprofittimes.com/report/millennials-value-everyday-social-good-above-cash-donations/.

Today's inheritors are not only receiving the most significant generational shift of assets in history, with trillions of dollars moving into the hands of the next gen, but many are horrified by it. Millennials have witnessed extreme financial inequality and are much more negative about wealth and the wealthy than their parents and grandparents.[12] They have been taught about the importance of diversity and inclusion and were encouraged not to accept institutions and leaders blindly. They lived through Occupy Wall Street, a recession with the majority of their peers in college taking on massive student debt and struggling to find jobs, the Me-Too Movement, Black Lives Matter and the COVID pandemic. Many reflect on how their family's fortune was made with disgust. They believe that it was created in part due to racial and gender discrimination and greed.

Despite many inheritors feeling uncomfortable being born into wealth, they are taking positive action. They are engaging in activism, impact investing, philanthropy, and purposeful entrepreneurship. A striking statistic is that 75 percent of millennials (born 1981–1996) describe themselves as philanthropists compared to 25 percent of baby boomers (born 1946–1964.)[13]

## Perceptions Post-Pandemic

Negative attitudes and stereotypes of wealth creators and inheritors increase as wealth inequality increases.

Wealth inequality has been growing for years, but COVID made the inequities more pronounced, obvious, and extreme. Lower and

---

[13]The Future of Philanthropy, 2021, Fidelity Charitable https://www.fidelitycharitable.org/content/dam/fc-public/docs/resources/2021-future-of-philanthropy-summary.pdf

middle-class families struggled with the loss of jobs, responsibility for caring for and educating children at home (those lucky to be able to work from home juggling both) and scraping by with (often criticized) stimulus checks.

White collar workers and wealth holders' investment portfolios soared, with many able to work from home, maintaining or growing income, and hiring help to care for and teach children—many from their second homes, while posting pictures on social media.

In 2020 and 2021, the American middle class (60 percent of U.S. household income) saw combined assets drop by approximately 27 percent—the lowest in 30 years. The middle class now holds a smaller share of US wealth than the top percent.[14] The total wealth of the top 1 percent increased by more than one-third during the pandemic.[15] The U.S. added 50 billionaires during the pandemic, and the total wealth of billionaires grew by $1.3 trillion—an increase of 44 percent.[16]

Around the world, the top 1 percent of wealth holders have captured nearly 20 times more global wealth than the bottom 50 percent of humanity.[17]

[14]Frank, Robert. "Soaring Markets Helped the Richest 1% Gain $6.5 Trillion in Wealth Last Year, According to the Fed." CNBC, April 1, 2022. https://www.cnbc.com/2022/04/01/richest-one-percent-gained-trillions-in-wealth-2021.html.

[15]Peterson-Withorn, Chase. "Forbes' 36th Annual World's Billionaires List: Facts And Figures 2022." Forbes, April 5, 2022. https://www.forbes.com/sites/chasewithorn/2022/04/05/forbes-36th-annual-worlds-billionaires-list-facts-and-figures-2022/?sh=430369f57e30Op.

[16]Peterson-Withorn, Chase. "Forbes' 36th Annual World's Billionaires List: Facts And Figures 2022." Forbes, April 5, 2022. https://www.forbes.com/sites/chasewithorn/2022/04/05/forbes-36th-annual-worlds-billionaires-list-facts-and-figures-2022/?sh=430369f57e30Op.

[17]Credit Suisse Global Wealthy report 2021.

## A Call for Change

Society is driving toward a cliff. History has taught us extreme financial inequality is not sustainable. Negative stereotypes and biases about being rich can and need to be changed for the benefit of the wealthy and the world.

We have the opportunity to do better. We all have a responsibility to do better.

The notion that family wealth is meant to be protected and kept in the family with no responsibility to use it to help others or reduce harm is unsustainable.

The next generation of wealth creators and inheritors is demanding more. More from the companies they buy from. More from looking for businesses that also have purpose and donate a portion of profits to the community and world. More from their careers, prioritizing working for inclusive, diverse, equitable companies who give back and share an alignment of values. More from non-profits—giving of time, talents, and resources, holding organizations accountable for the change they wish to see in the world. More from their wealth managers, with a dramatic rise in demand for impact investment options, ESG (environmental, social, and governance) metrics, and philanthropic services. And more from their family office than asset growth, protection, and tax mitigation. They are expanding their focus to include individual well-being, family flourishing, lifelong learning, and activating financial resources to protect the world and ensure human rights for the entire human family.

Wealth holders and family offices have the opportunity and responsibility to manage "family wealth" using the definition James Hughes introduced us to 20 years ago: that a family's wealth comprises human capital, intellectual capital, social capital, spiritual capital, and financial capital.[18] We also have the opportunity to enact his idea that the best use of a family's financial money is to nurture others. And we have the opportunity and responsibility to strive for conscious capitalism recognizing that the innate potential of business is to create value *and* positively impact the world.

In addition to redefining wealth, what if we redefine "return" to encompass more than just financial returns? What if it included an analysis of how an investment impacts humanity, society, the planet, and our spirit? What if investments have an impact, and we have the opportunity and responsibility to strive to ensure the effect is positive—if not for us, then for future generations?

What if wealth was defined entirely differently? What if the words that come to mind when we think of wealth focus on well-being, such as connection, community, relationships, peace, giving, and love? We can change our reality if we change the definition and our attitudes, biases, and stereotypes.

In conclusion, we are living in unique times which create opportunities to be change agents.

---

[18]Hughes Jr, J. E. (2010). Family Wealth: Keeping It in the Family--How Family Members and Their Advisers Preserve Human, Intellectual, and Financial Assets for Generations. John Wiley & Sons.

## Reflection Questions

- How sustainable is the growing financial inequality in our society?

- Given we all share this one planet, what responsibilities do we have to each other? To earth?

- What should be expected from the 1 percent?

- What is the responsibility of family offices and family office professionals? Doctors must intervene if behaviors are causing harm (smoking, violence, abuse.) If wealth adversely affects individuals, relationships, the community, and the environment, are wealth managers negligent?

- What can wealth holders and the advisors who serve them do to shift the paradigm and refocus and redefine wealth to go beyond money?

- What if we focused on the human family rather than blood connected family?

- What would it mean if tomorrow we had a more holistic approach by family offices where all types of capital were assessed with the same focus and expertise that financial capital is today?

# Family Office Relevancy: Doing What's Asked For and What's Needed

### By Jim Coutré

**Jeffery's risk-taking paid off time and time again.** Unorthodox decisions rewarded him with financial capital, which grew faster than he could reinvest on his own. So, he founded a family office to deploy that capital and build multigenerational wealth for his growing family. Over the decades, the office evolved as an investment powerhouse supporting Jeffery's newer real estate and direct investment passions.

Electrified by the returns the office was earning, Jeffery was blindsided and furious when his children informed him they wanted their piece of the pie to take elsewhere. Neither of the siblings knew what the family office did. Their father was absorbed in his priorities, and the family office's investment professionals had dismissed the siblings for as long as anyone could remember. One was eager for genuine financial autonomy and couldn't wait to move his money into his college roommate's Wirehouse group. There, he thought he would finally get the attention and respect he wanted and be unencumbered in his ability to invest in entrepreneurial ventures. And the other was anxious to separate herself from her brother, who continued to make bad life choices and business decisions that dragged down everyone around him. This was true despite her failure to launch, grounded in a lifetime of behavioral health struggles.

A useful family office delivers on the operational needs of the family in the important investing, legal, and tax issues facing the family. But offices that do only that are more likely to eventually be dismissed by family members who don't see them as relevant to their daily lives or the lives they want, including the broader hopes and aspirations beyond financial success.

The factors that keep a family office constrained to the core operational needs are grounded in most design flaws discussed in this book. This includes the family's lack of a unifying sense of purpose, the lack of diverse thinking in the office's start-up or evolution, and the relatively narrow technical expertise held by the professionals employed to shape the office. As important as the risk of being dismissed by the family is, these narrowly defined offices are a lost opportunity to more holistically develop the health and capacity families require to make a decision that considers their impact on the world around them.

Attending to the family's many practical needs is only one component in serving the family's strategic needs or the factors supporting multigenerational success. Addressing higher-order systemic issues (health, self-activation, effective decision-making, family thriving, etc.) requires a family office to achieve and maintain *relevancy* over time, one of the most challenging yet rewarding qualities a family office can have.

This chapter will explore relevancy as a concept and suggest pathways to move toward a more relevant office.

The factors or design flaws that keep an office contained to core operational functions include the following:

## Offices seldom capture a family's unifying sense of purpose or vision.

- Many families encounter tangible needs long before they recognize their intangible needs or can articulate their qualitative capital goals that can make an office transformative.

- Families tend to focus and make progress on the things that others are holding them accountable for. Tax returns need to be filed. Finding joy doesn't have a due date.

## Office startups lack diversity in thought and find safety in replicating the norm.

- Professionals who have never started an office (and typically come from risk-averse professions) gather insight from and follow the lead of peers who look, sound, and think like them.

- Professionals without experience in starting an office typically come from a risk-averse professional field. They will understandably want to stay within the standard deviation of the peer offices they have talked with.

## Offices are primarily created by technical specialists, and when you're a hammer, everything looks like a nail.

- Professionals, who most families will defer to, naturally lean on their expertise, viewing priorities and decision-making through the lens of what they know best and what they assume the family wants as they were hired for that expertise.

- Families rarely hire professionals with a deep understanding of family systems or dedicated to family thriving. Financial wealth dominates the discourse and culture.

## Office startups can be shaped by unproductive or unhealthy narratives.

- Family offices are often approached as a cost center rather than an investment in a family or individual.

- Family offices are structured around a generational hierarchy where the few at the top make decisions for the many at the bottom.

## Professionals are not family members.

- Professionals creating offices to serve multiple family members rarely know those family members and that it is healthy for them to stay connected through an office.

- Professionals tend to start building in "do-er mode" rather than "strategic-thinker mode."

- Professionals are held accountable for specific, measurable metrics and will focus on this, even if at the expense of more critical, less quantifiable outcomes.

**Family members are not professionals.**

- Very few family members come to the table with the familiarity of diverse family office models. When they do, it is typically a small, idiosyncratic data set from a few peers.

- Decisions around keeping family members connected are rarely co-created by those family members.

## Understanding Relevancy

Relevancy—the real and perceived sense of connection between a family and its family office—is the key to unlocking the potential and sustainability of a family office. It requires a combination of *connection*, *significance*, and *value* delivered *over time*. These qualities are mainly intangible, yet they are powerful in their presence or absence.

A family's sense of *connection* to its office derives from its comfort, relatability, and trust in the office and its staff. *Significance* grows from a sense that the office is beneficial in what matters and takes issues in the family seriously. *Value* reflects a family's deep appreciation of the office's services and that expectations are met and exceeded. Value delivered *over time* underscores that relevancy goes beyond any given moment and must be constantly reinforced.

Offices aren't required to be relevant. It's easy to find an active office that, for example, plays one specific role for one person. Or to find a wealth creator who wants a bare-bones office because she has no interest in staffing an office "so someone can walk my granddaughter's poodle." Experience shows that offices that are not relevant are eventually abandoned. While abandonment can be a slow process that plays out over the years, it also happens more abruptly. For example, it can occur when family members "cash out" when the founder passes, when one of the family's branches revolts and turns to litigation, or when some family members drive out a long-serving executive. There is nothing wrong with closing an office or encouraging family members to start their own offices—when that is the intention. When it happens *despite* intentions, however, it opens the family up to unnecessary risk and conflict.

## The Benefits of a Relevant Office

Working toward relevancy has many positive impacts on the family, such as:

**Helping the family thrive outside of financial capital.** When family members feel connected to their executives, those executives are better positioned to support or even nudge families in their work to pursue the nonfinancial success of individual members and the collective family. As Scott Peppet has said, "For a family office to ignore the long-term health of the family is to uphold the ruse that someone else is doing that work. If not the family office, then who? If not the family office, then why a family office?"[19]

**Fostering continuity.** Families constantly evolve, sometimes in disruptive ways. An office that remains relevant is better positioned to help navigate rocky transitions, lowering the risk of conflict or collapse.

---

[19]Scott Peppet, "Do Family Offices Care About Family Capital? Family Firm Institute (Aug. 18, 2021 webinar.

**Keeping the family safe**. Complying with security protocols to move assets, plan for family emergencies, or maintain cybersecurity will be more likely when family members listen to an office they consider relevant.

**Receiving excellence from their office.** When a family is more knowledgeable about and engaged with the office, they will more likely receive the service and execution excellence they are looking for.

As important, a relevant office can positively impact the world beyond the family.

**Recognizing the impact on the broader world.** The world's wealthiest families have an oversized impact, which can be a positive or a negative for society and the planet. Family members and family systems who are not healthy, not self-aware, and not high functioning will have a much harder time seeing or caring about how their decisions impact others. A relevant office is more likely to engage in these higher-order systemic needs and help the family move towards their goals for individual growth, health, and thriving—a foundation for thoughtful decision-making. As Don Opatrny says, "When the wealthy are healthy, the whole world wins."[20]

Are enterprising families obliged to invest in the health and functioning of family members so they can make decisions that consider their impact on others? Many will say "no." We don't hold the wealthy accountable when their decisions negatively impact people or the

---

[20]D. Opatrny, personal communication, April 5, 2022.

planet (for example, exploitive industries, unsafe workplaces, pollution, excessive carbon footprint.) We may applaud the philanthropic deeds of some families, and we may disapprove of the lifestyle choices of other families. Yet, neither that appreciation nor disapproval impacts those families' ability to operate as freely as they want.

"With great wealth comes great responsibility," the adage says, but who is policing the responsibility part of that equation? Driving an automobile comes with great responsibility; irresponsible and impaired driving takes the lives of other motorists or pedestrians. As a society, we hold drivers accountable for taking driving lessons, earning a license, and obeying the rules of the road, which we enforce through costly tickets or loss of license. We require no such training or licensure for family members behind the wheel of multi-billion-dollar enterprises or investment portfolios. It's not hard to find examples of multi-billion-dollar enterprises that have had a far more significant impact—and been far deadlier—than a single automobile. Fortunately, pursuing a relevant family office that, by definition, engages and supports higher-order needs increases the chances that family members and family systems will produce decisions that consider their holistic impact even if positive social impact is not the stated goal.

## Four Pathways for Moving a Family Office Towards Greater Relevance

A relevant family office can be built by going beyond stated needs and uncovering the family's actual needs. This involves using a relevancy-focused process to invent or evolve, staying vigilant to confusion between office relevancy and personal relevancy, and evaluating progress towards relevancy indicators.

## Respond to the family's actual needs and stated needs.

In some ways, relevancy is akin to the financial industry's distinction between a basic suitability standard and a fiduciary "best interests" standard. Family offices may do what a family requests in the many tactical areas that a family finds onerous yet necessary—mostly tax, investment, insurance, and estate planning activities. But a genuinely relevant family office goes beyond these to what all parties determine to be in the best long-term interests of the family.

Families are good at expressing the needs they see at their fingertips. These *stated needs* are often the foundation upon which family offices are started: "we need to invest this cash"; "we need to file our taxes." Moving beyond these stated needs to uncover actual needs can be difficult. Comprised of individuals with different life stages, personalities, philosophies, levels of expertise, and vocations, families can have wildly disparate opinions about what they require and who should help them. They may not know what other family offices do or how offices serve other families. They may not have identified shared family goals or goals for the development of individual family members—or fundamentally may still be figuring out what it means to be a non-traditional family. They also tend to rely on professionals with specific technical expertise to tell them what they need. This complexity creates an incentive to narrow focus; responding to stated needs with suitable solutions does create satisfaction with the family office—and an assumption that the office is doing what it is meant to do.

More complex than pointing to these tangible, logistical needs is for families to articulate their *actual needs*, the pursuit of which will make their office more relevant. Families who strive to uncover their actual needs see the complex connections between operational choices and long-term outcomes, leading to solutions that are much more in the family's best interest. For example, a family who wants to preserve financial wealth through the generations will likely invest heavily in estate planning and tax management. However, efficient tax planning won't prepare an inheritor not to be derailed when becoming the beneficiary of a significant trust. The *stated* need is for capital preservation and estate planning. The *actual* need is for healthy, prepared family members capable of using financial capital granted by the estate plan to enhance their lives.

Stated and actual needs play out not just in the "what" of a family office but also in the "how." For example, many family offices are built around a desire for efficiency, low overhead, and extreme confidentiality; these are the stated needs. But for those families who do not want subsequent generations to break the family office apart (for security, continuity, or investment reasons), their offices will also need to improve and evolve continually. Actual needs, in this case, may be finding more modern ways to operate and innovating new services that reflect the times. And to meet them, family office executives may need time to network with peers, be exposed to other offices, solutions, and vendors, or carve out an R&D budget to learn about new trends or macro shifts that will affect the family. These are all things that are not comfortably supported when an office's stated needs only include "efficiency, low overhead, and extreme confidentiality."

Jill Barber gave us a great example in this book when discussing how she could have changed the technical distribution requirements of a trust as requested by the trust creators. Instead, she slowed down and reflected on the situation, uncovering the actual need to address the emotional weight the trust creators were carrying.

Stated needs versus actual needs can also be a lens to examine the existential question of "why a family office at all?" Family office leader and family member Scott Peppet has posed this question to his family: "In the coming year, would you rather have slightly better tax preparation in your life or more joy?" Despite the answer always being "more joy," the actual need of the family, few offices invest anywhere near the resources in joy as they do in the stated need of tax preparation.

Other chapters in this book discuss moving beyond stated to actual needs, even if not using those terms. Paul Carbone describes the benefits of shifting from purely financial, passive investors (stated need of investing) to more active deployers of the family's capital (actual need of retaining a family's sense of purpose.) Andrew Keyt writes about the actual need of a family to take emotional ownership for establishing a sense of purpose, meaning, and vision for the family office. Mary Duke's and Stacy Allred's ideas about the family office as a learning and development tool to help the family thrive are built on the understanding that an office that only pursues the stated, tactical needs will not deliver on the family's actual need for long-term personal and financial success.

## Use a relevancy-focused process for creating or evolving an office.

Examining actual needs is at the core of working towards a more relevant office. A relevancy-focused approach when building an office from scratch brings the advantage of working from a clean slate, yet offices can tackle the work at any time and through a major pivot or more gradual course corrections. Some families use targeted conversations during family meetings. Others hire consultants to interview family members and facilitate decision-making. Still others intentionally engage visionary executives with high emotional intelligence or dedicated family learning and development professionals. And some families make space for such conversations around the dinner table or in the car. Experience shows that a more formal process helps by carving out time to work on the issues and by holding everyone involved more accountable for delivering on the work. However, for some family cultures, doing something more casual is better than not trying.

Regardless of how formal or informal an office wants to make its process towards relevancy, a good starting point is reflecting on why the office is the way that it is—or for family office start-ups, reflecting on why family offices typically become what they become. Although others can help facilitate this reflection process, the family must find its answer and own it. The family-professional partnership is critical to any effort to achieve relevancy. Neither party can be expected to bring about change without the support and active participation of the other.

Choosing the best process to pursue greater relevancy depends on factors like the life stage of the office, natural inflection points such as leadership or generational transitions, the family's appetite to embark on a process, and the bandwidth office professionals have for the work involved. Leveraging strategic or non-linear thinking in addition to more linear, tactical thinking, can prove challenging but worth pursuing for a family office start-up or when tackling as a significant inflection point.

Design thinking is one option for pushing strategic, non-linear thinking to the forefront. Design thinking has been used for years in various contexts and is commonly associated with The Hasso Plattner Institute of Design at Stanford, widely known as the d.school. The d.school has produced numerous resources that family offices reference. It has even partnered with the Forge Community to help single family office executives understand and apply design thinking to all aspects of their work. (Family members and single family office executives can engage in the Forge Community of family offices through www. ForgeCommunity.com to access these resources.) Design thinking is a nonlinear process that zigzags iteratively in multiple learning, prototyping, and testing waves. It's a perfect foil to the linear functions that create offices that do one thing well, remaining irrelevant to the rest of the family's lives.

The Stanford d.school design thinking process consists of five stages:

1. Seek a deep understanding of the stakeholders.

2. Define or *re-define* the challenge or opportunity at hand.

3. Generate a wide range and large quantity of ideas.

4. Quickly construct prototypes that can be reacted to.

5. Test and tweak.

At every stage, something new will be discovered, and as such, it is common to jump backward and forwards between various stages. (Please visit https://dschool.stanford.edu for a graphic illustration of this process.)

Through the lens of a family office start up or re-invention, these stages might look like this:

**Empathize**. Learn as much as you can. Yes, talk to other families and look at other offices, but also invest time getting to know all the impacted people (not just the wealth creator or decision maker.) Capture stated needs, but also pursue deeper levels of inquiry to learn about who the family is and who they want to be, including their goals and visions beyond financial capital.

**Redefine**. Resist the temptation to solve only the most pressing tangible need. Think broadly and articulate opportunities that can be realized through an office that is more relevant to the lives of more of the family and see this process as an investment in the long-term health and success of the family however they define it.

**Ideate.** Brainstorm all the ways the family could be supported regardless of whether the family office will ultimately deliver on them. Not everything a family needs must be delivered through the family office, but the process of articulating those needs and wants will make it more likely they will be addressed in some form at some time.

**Prototype.** What role could the office play for family members? What might the office do? How might the office do it? Prototype beyond the assumed or historical single family office model, exploring, for example, how a virtual family office, private trust company, or multi-family office (commercial or non-commercial) model might work for the family.

**Test.** Review with impacted family members and supporting professionals. What is embraced and why? What is dismissed or missing and why?

A design thinking process is effective when starting a family office and when there is an appetite for more concentrated change, yet a more subtle or gradual move towards relevance is also an option for offices. Simply creating space to talk about the issues—with family office professionals, a board, a family council, a rising generation, or individual family members—can be effective in bringing about change.

## Reflection Questions for Family Office Executives

- Is the office on track to deliver connection, significance, and value throughout the years as the family evolves?

- How does the family want to show up in the world? How does the family define a successful life?

- How might the family articulate what they want from a relevant family office? Has this been asked of them?

- What factors might bias or constrain how the family articulates relevancy?

- Beyond the family's stated needs, do the family's long-term goals or current reality suggest additional areas where the office might provide value?

- Do I as an executive have blind spots, keeping me or the office from maximizing our relevance to the family?

- Is the office staffed intentionally to ensure meaningful connections with all family members?

- When should I be a master of tasks and when do I need to be a visionary? How much time should I spend being each?

- What indicators might I monitor to alert me I'm moving towards being over-responsive, operationally opaque, or blurring lines between serving and enabling family members? From whom and how can I and the SFO staff get feedback on this?

- Realistically, at what point is my own relevancy to the office or family likely to wane?

## Reflection Questions for Family Members

- How do I want to show up in the world? What is the life I want for myself and my family?

- How would I articulate what a relevant office looks like? How might others articulate it?

- What factors might bias or constrain how my family thinks about connection, significance, and value over time?

- Are the service demands and expectations for the office aligned with how my family defines relevancy?

- Are there multigenerational goals or ambitions for my family which are not being supported by the office? Are there goals that are potentially being undermined by the office?

- How might the focus or experience of our executives shape the office or its relevancy?

- In what situations do we need a master of tasks running our office and when are we best served by a visionary?

- Do our executives have the time and resources to keep an eye on the horizon?

- How might the family support our family office executives, so they are best positioned to meet the long-term needs of our family?

- How do we each know if we are fulfilling the role our family wants us to play? How will we know when it is time to change our role? From whom and how can I get feedback on this?

Stay alert to how an individual's quest for relevancy can get in the way of an office's relevancy.

This desire for personal relevancy or the confusion between office relevancy and personal relevancy by any one player in the system can create a number of negative consequences. This can occur both with non-family executives and with family leaders who work with the family office. An overly tight grip on personal relevancy by either side, whether driven by ego or by the best intentions, is likely to produce some combination of false relevancy, exclusion, a black box around service, and dependency.

**False relevancy**. Executives needing to stay relevant themselves often double down on the expertise or tasks they know best. This is a concept that Jill Barber and Greg McCann delve into in their chapter. "I do X really well, so I'm going to make sure to always engage the family around X and orient the office around X." This narrow focus breeds security and praise. But it keeps executives from seeing how the office could better serve the family. It can also keep them stuck in a task-based or managerial role rather than a more visionary or CEO role where they are continually evolving the office with the family.

On the family side, a family leader clinging to their role can compromise the office if they fall out of touch with important strategic goals, especially if they refuse the help of others as conditions evolve. In one office struggling to retain talent under the stresses of constant conflict, a family leader ultimately was confronted by an executive about their imperial manner: "I understand it may not feel like you are the king when you are not surrounded by your court, but the world—and our workforce—has changed." Though harsh, this led to a more collaborative style which then greatly reduced staff turnover.

**Failing to include others.** In an effort to make themselves personally valuable in the family's eyes, executives may work in a bubble or run an office more like a dictatorship than a democracy. They fail to engage the broader office team in serving the family or determining how the office might innovate. They may also fail to engage the family or ignore what the family wants in favor of their own perspectives.

In one example combining these elements, an executive in a newly unembedded family office struggled to engage the family's interest when showcasing the tax benefits she had developed. Though hired for her tax expertise, she grew frustrated and distant when the family just didn't seem excited about her accomplishments. She failed to hear how the family's operating business has always been broadly values-driven, a focus that carried over to the new family office. Had this executive listened to and understood others in the operating business and office, she would have learned her tax-centric approach was unlikely to generate much excitement despite the benefits.

Family members can also be guilty of pushing their own agendas or positions, ignoring collaboration with the office in favor of their personal utility. This can become entrenched when there are disincentives (i.e., loss of access or employment) keeping office staff or other family members from being truly honest with the offender. In any of these situations, diminishing one person's 'command and control' style creates room for effective teams to emerge, a prerequisite for the office to remain relevant over time.

**Creating a black box of services**. Driven by a heartfelt desire to serve, many executives believe relevancy is defined by delivering whatever the family wants, whenever the family wants it, without ever showing the complexity required to do it. Unfortunately, this can backfire severely. It can train a family to assume the office can do anything, independent of the individuals involved, thereby making everyone a replaceable commodity. Moreover, the family can learn not to value the executive's role, accept reasonable pushback, or appreciate boundaries between work and employees' personal lives.

Creating a "black box" system that seemingly can do everything keeps family members from understanding what the office does and the costs involved, which is not an insignificant factor in choosing what an office should be offering. Long-term, this risks a kind of magical thinking that can hide escalating problems in the sustainability of the office itself or its services. It also undermines the family's educated participation in the evolution of the office. Ironically, being transparent about how things operate and involving the family in setting realistic human boundaries ultimately brings the office and family closer.

**Impeding by enabling dependency.** Jumping on a moment's notice to serve a family member can feel great to the office under the guise of being "highly responsive" and seemingly relevant. Yet, this do-anything attitude can prevent family members from earning the skills or resilience the family wants them to have, such as the 30-something stranded at an airport because they have no idea how to navigate a commercial flight change.

At the leadership level, keeping oneself indispensable can turn from relevance to impediment, as when a long-serving executive says they are committed to succession yet stays involved in running the office rather than making room for the incoming leader. Similarly, family members in governance may cling to relevancy long after the family needs them to transition involvement to others.

The line between helpful participation and getting in the way can be blurry. To combat this, family members must become engaged owners who can work together with their offices to decide which actions are responsive and which are not counterproductive, then periodically revisit the issue as conditions change over time.

## Measure progress on common elements found in a relevant office.

In looking across offices that feel relevant, several common threads can be seen. While the nine elements described below don't suggest how to achieve a relevant office, their absence will indicate a lack of relevancy. Thus, there is value in evaluating each informally or, better yet, creating a scorecard to understand progress. Gathering data and assessing progress can be approached informally through self-reflection, by querying family members, or more formally through a family council, or by hiring an outside consultant. Each approach comes with advantages and disadvantages that should be explored in the context of the given situation.

**Trust.** Everything circles back to trust. If the family trusts the office and there's a strong, foundational relationship built on trust, there are more opportunities to offer recommendations and/or course corrections to help maintain relevancy to the family. And while personal trust is good, "professionalized" trust, a more informed trust based on engagement, is even better.

**Service.** Services can build relevancy if the family's needs and wants are met while executives keep a wary eye on the potential downside of "black boxing," commoditization, and family member-enabling.

**Rapport.** Suppose a family member isn't comfortable with office executives. In that case, that family member will always stay hands-off, and it's hard to build trust without rapport, especially since so much of relevancy is emotional. (Remember, perceived relevancy is relevancy.)

**Listening.** The key component here is seeking an understanding of the whole family, not just the loudest voices or the biggest votes. Feedback needs to be sought, not avoided, as messy as that might become.

**Communication.** It's all about transparency and ties directly to rapport, listening, and trust.

**Executional excellence.** None of the drivers mentioned above matter if you can't execute flawlessly.

**Space for foresight.** No leader can see what might be emerging on the horizon if their eyes are always down, focusing on execution excellence.

**Ability to speak truth to power.** Some "trusted advisors" have earned that title simply because the family "trusts" that they won't push back or raise uncomfortable topics. This does not make anyone relevant. Often, more value can be created by explaining an unpopular decision to the family rather than accommodating an off-target request.

**Innovation, agility, and flexibility.** Even if only glacially, the family is continually evolving. Those executives who can react and stay slightly ahead of the family's evolution are more likely to ensure their relevancy over the long haul.

## Time for Bolder Action?

Given the opportunity and need for a healthier, high-functioning family that comes from a relevant office supporting these higher-order actual needs, is there a role for the professional and citizen communities to encourage, inspire or push a family office towards relevancy?

Could a new social contract be established between communities and wealthy families to trade privilege or operational freedom for proof of learning and development for family members instead of the informal agreement today that simply hopes wealthy families give some money to charities?

Taking it a step further, could a new social contract require proof of training along the lines of a driver's education and a driving test before a driving license is granted? Similarly, could society look to influence the professionals surrounding wealthy families? Like professional continuing education credits for lawyers, family office professionals could be required to study the basics of family systems and human development. The goal could be not necessarily to become experts in the topics but at least to understand the importance of bringing health and higher functioning into families that wield such power.

To add teeth to social contracts, could we not explore requiring proof of training and development, published impact reporting, or a family office version of the B-corporation designation in exchange for the right to operate as freely as family offices do today rather than face additional levels of limitation, oversight, reporting or tax? While it's hard to imagine the family office field not banding together to oppose any limitations or requirements, perhaps concessions would be made, or members who understand the unsustainability of our current system would be willing to lead the charge. It is not too dissimilar from some of the family leadership we see today in the impact investing space.

Achievable? Pointless? Worth a little bit of exploration? Rewriting a social contract that demands more for society and the planet from the world's most powerful families would be no easy task, but in the statement often attributed to Schopenhauer, "All truth passes through three stages. First, it is ridiculed. Second, it is violently opposed. Third, it is accepted as being self-evident."[21]

The benefits of a relevant family office are far-reaching. They are grounded in benefit to individual family members. A relevant family office is an investment in them, an investment when done right, that empowers rather than enables and is capable of supporting the family's most closely cherished goals which often include the quest for meaning and the growth of self-reliance, achievement of satisfaction. A relevant family office protects the family, better positions it for any multi-generational goals the family may have and creates a platform for the family to thrive beyond financial capital. Greater family thriving produces individuals and families more capable of understanding how their decisions will impact others and the world around them. This, in turn, can create decision-making by the world's most powerful and influential families that ripples out in more positive ways worldwide.

---

[21]All Truth Passes through Three Stages. First, It Is Ridiculed. Second, It Is Violently Opposed. Third, It Is Accepted as Being Self-Evident.," n.d. https://quoteinvestigator.com/2016/11/18/truth-stages/.

# The Transformative Family Office

## By Andrew Keyt

**"We need your help.** We have three family board members who will step down in the next three to five years, and no one in the next generation is ready to fill that role. Heck, we are even having trouble getting next-generation members to attend family meetings," said Sara Peterson, the newly minted CEO of an 80-year-old family office. Serving over 100 family members, as only the third leader of this family office, Sara faced the challenge of re-envisioning a family office that had been built to grow and manage the wealth of the Jones family.[22]

Founded in 1942 in Denver, Colorado, the Jones Family office was established by Bill, Jay, and Laura Jones after the sale of their family manufacturing business for $50 million. With wise investment in public equities and real estate, the family office managed over $1.6 billion in assets. While the Jones family office had achieved tremendous financial success, the family had become increasingly passive over the years.

---

[22] This is a composite case based on work with many family offices over a number of years.

At the inception of the family office, Bill, Jay, and Laura were highly engaged, working to ensure that the assets generated by the sale of their family business were managed responsibly. Their focus was on diversifying their investments, developing trust structures to protect that wealth, and developing an infrastructure to manage the complexity of their taxes. The eleven members of the second generation of the Jones family office were also highly engaged in the family office. Still, they focused more on their personal affairs and investments. Three members of the second generation worked in the family office managing real estate and investments, four worked to establish a family foundation and a philanthropic mission, and three used family financial capital to start their own businesses.

Through the 1970s and 80s, the family grew and expanded well beyond Denver, pursued more and more divergent interests, and gradually came to see the family office primarily as the administrators of their trusts and manager of their investments. They had little to no understanding of how the family office was run and governed and how strategic decisions were made. The annual family meetings were a lengthy report on the performance of their different investments with little to no discussion about how the family office was run.

Over time, the family outsourced more and more decision-making and responsibility to their family office team. Eventually, most family members' only focus was on the performance of their accounts and how much was available to fund their personal needs. There was little to no focus on what was happening within the family office; they had outsourced the ownership of the family office to the professional staff.

Recently 15 family members had pulled their assets out of the family office and moved them to be managed by a prominent New York-based multi-family office. They reported wanting more autonomy in managing their assets and an office closer to where they lived on the east coast.

The problems facing the Jones family office—a fragmented and disengaged ownership group—resulted from the typical design flaws we have explored throughout this book. Like many family offices, the Jones family built their family office primarily around their financial objectives of protecting the assets generated by the sale of their family business. In establishing their family office, they overlooked the need to build a unifying sense of purpose and meaning to direct what they wanted to do with their financial capital. They staffed their office with talented technical specialists and gave them financially focused goals, but they didn't establish a focus for the family office beyond just financial returns. While the family was very involved in the beginning, the family office didn't spend any time investing in the family. They didn't invest in the growth and development of the rising generation; and over time, the family became more disengaged to the point that there was a widespread lack of understanding of the family office by the family members.

The result is a family that sees themselves more as clients of the family office than owners. With a client mentality, family members think about what the family office can do for them. And that threatens the long-term sustainability of the Jones family office as an entity. A family that truly wants to build an organization that can sustain the test of time needs to think about building a foundation for the family office that can survive for this generation and beyond.

In this chapter, we will explore how a family can start addressing these design flaws by taking emotional ownership to establish a sense of purpose and vision for the family office that taps into the family's values and passions. To do this, we will look at the research on the sustainability of long-term family businesses and explore the implications for the family office as a family enterprise. We will explore the importance of cultivating a sense of ownership, unity, and family cohesion that fosters a sense of purpose and commitment to the family's long-term success and enterprise. We will explore how a family, in partnership with their family office leadership, can create a transformative family office that manages the family's financial, human, social, intellectual, and spiritual capital.

## How Family Office Design Flaws Lead to Passive and Disconnected Ownership

As Jill Shipley shared earlier, the families that create family offices most often move from a highly illiquid business that they are engaged in, to a business that is liquid, passive, and that they have little to no experience with. This might include, for example, managing investments, venture capital, private equity, and family services.

As they shift to a new form of family enterprise, they often overlook their commitment to the processes of ownership that made their family businesses successful (Boards of Directors, regular family meetings, and strategic planning) that created a sense of purpose and direction for the family ownership group.

As families make this transition from a business they know (the family business of origin) to a company that they don't know (the family office), as Jim Coutré identified earlier, they focus the design of their family office around their stated needs (investment management, tax strategy, financial administration) rather than their actual needs (establishing a sense of purpose and meaning for the family office, establishing a vision that meets not just the financial needs of the family but also the long term needs to cultivate a sense of cohesion and responsible ownership within the family).

In forsaking the actual needs, families often don't make the same commitment to one of the critical responsibilities of ownership, developing an effective governance system that provides accountability. Sustaining any family enterprise requires good governance in both the family and the family office. One of the primary roles of governance is to give a sense of accountability and direction. A family office needs to develop a robust governance system that cultivates a strong sense of purpose and mission that provide a holistic understanding of direction for both the family owners and the non-family members supporting the family. The family needs to play a central part in the governance process. Strong governance that brings objectivity, diversity, and broad perspective. Key elements of this governance should include:

- Objective and diverse participation on the family office board.

- Regular family meetings to work on family cohesion and connection.

- A holistic strategic planning process that engages and aligns the family and the family office team.

## Impact of the Design Flaws

The outcome of these design flaws is financially functional models for family offices that don't inspire any sense of meaning and purpose for the family. These offices are fully capable of managing the financial capital of the family. Still, they don't create a long-term sense of purpose that will keep the family engaged owners of the family office as a family enterprise. Some examples of what these types of offices might look like include:

**The embedded family office.** Often team members inside the family business serve the needs of the family. This is the beginning of a family office. The CFO does family taxes, admin support manages family properties, and the general counsel manages family partnerships outside the business.

**The financial family office.** The family office is primarily designed as a business to manage wealth for a family, sometimes morphing into a multi-family office. Its primary purpose is to produce investment returns for clients and owners.

**The administrative family office.** A family establishes a family office and staff primarily to serve the administrative needs of the family, including tax filing, bill paying, and real estate management. Perhaps also managing investment managers from other service providers.

Because these prototypical models for a family office are created primarily with a financial purpose in mind, the structure and staffing of the office reflect that focus on financial capital. There is excellent legal, tax, and financial talent in the family office but no talent devoted to fostering a sense of purpose and emotional connection among the family. These types of offices often develop a mentality of trying to take care of every family need and solving every problem for the family. The result is that this creates a sense of entitlement and passivity in the family, robbing them of real opportunities for them to grow and develop their sense of ownership and responsibility.

## Sustaining the Family Office as a Family Enterprise

So how can we overcome these design flaws to create a family office that will survive the test of time? We need to look no further than the research into the long-term sustainability of family businesses.

Research into the sustainability of family businesses by Dr. Torsten Pieper and Dr. Joe Astrachan has found that while financial success is a longevity factor, family cohesion is the defining factor in family business longevity.[23] Their research looked at families that had sustained themselves across hundreds of years and found that family cohesion was the critical factor in sustaining a family business over time.

The researchers identified several dimensions of Family Cohesion, including Family Emotional, Business Emotional, Family Financial, and Business Financial Cohesion. The financial dimensions of cohesion are intuitive to most people. Business cohesion occurs when the financial success of the business generates cohesion in the family (for example, dividends and capital growth). Family financial cohesion is

---

[23] Pieper, T. M., & Astrachan, J. H. (2008). Mechanisms to assure family business cohesion: Guidelines for family business leaders and their families. Kennesaw, GA: Cox Family Enterprise Center.

when the family uses their financial resources to support and help each other, which creates cohesion (for example, paying for education and assisting with down payments on houses). It is intuitive to most of us that financial success and financial resources can help increase family cohesion. Still, these researchers found that the financial dimensions of cohesion were necessary but not sufficient for long-term survival. This means financial success alone won't lead to a long-lasting family enterprise.

These researchers found that family emotional and business cohesion correlated with stable family enterprises. They describe family emotional cohesion as a basic sense of connection, affiliation, and belonging that comes from our relationship as family members and business emotional cohesion as cohesion that comes from a sense of pride in what the businesses are doing and the impact that they are having in the world. I would assert that these are the essential components of emotional ownership.

This research supports the idea that a financially focused family office will likely fail to focus on building a sense of connection and affiliation amongst the family or a sense of pride and identity in what the family office is doing in the world. Because many offices focus on passive investments, they lose the opportunity to capture the pride and identity that comes from owning and operating a business that makes a real difference in its people, products, and communities. In a subsequent chapter, Paul Carbone will share how families can use the direct investing model to recapture the family legacy that may have been lost in establishing the family office.

But building family and business emotional cohesion won't just happen on its own. The growth in the complexity of the family over time requires that the family makes family cohesion a key objective of both the family and the family office.

When a family develops a true sense of cohesion, they create a sense of emotional ownership over the purpose and direction of the family enterprise. In their seminal work on Emotional Ownership, Åsa Björnberg & Nigel Nicholson define emotional ownership as a sense of closeness and belonging to the family business (or, in this case, the family office.)[24] In psychological terms, we might call this the emotional "attachment" level to the entity and what it can be. In the words of Nicholson and Björnberg, "this is more than just a warm fuzzy glow—it penetrates below the surface of the mind into the identity of the person who experiences emotional ownership. It is something to do with the subject (the family member) as well as the object (the business/family office)." In essence, emotional ownership moves the individual beyond just their legal rights and responsibilities to the entity to have a sense of emotional responsibility for the organization that becomes a part of their identity. They move from thinking about what the Family Office can do to serve them to what they can do to ensure the value of this family office now and for the future generation.

Why is this emotional ownership important to a Family Office? When family members care about the family office and what it does, they are more likely to sacrifice for the greater good. They develop an approach to preserving the family entity that Pieper and Astrachan

---

[24] Björnberg, Å., & Nicholson, N. (2012). Emotional ownership: The next generation's relationship with the family firm. Family business review, 25(4), 374-390.

(2008) describe as "Favoring preservation and collective service over consumption and individual, self-serving behavior." This leads to a family member who is not just using the resources of the family office for their own purpose. They are also thinking about sustaining and growing the resources of the family office for the greater good of the family, the employees, and the community. Emotional ownership, in many ways, is a commitment to maintaining the relevancy of the family office, as identified by Jim Coutré in Chapter 2.

## Creating Cohesion: Moving Beyond the Focus on Just Financial Capital

The prototypical family office structures identified above serve the technical and financial needs of the family, but they don't cultivate a sense of ownership, unity, and family cohesion. Financial success alone isn't a "reason for being" that will inspire the rising generation to build a sense of ownership and stewardship of the family office. It won't create a sense of emotional ownership.

To create family cohesion and a sense of emotional ownership, a family must wrestle with what they see as the purpose of their wealth (see Jill Shipley's chapter) and realize that financial capital isn't the only form of capital they are putting out into the world. In his book *Family Wealth—Keeping it in the Family*, Jay Hughes identifies four additional sources of family capital.[25] In addition to financial capital, Hughes identifies human, intellectual, social, and spiritual capital as additional resources to increase the sense of wealth and well-being of the family.

---

[25] Hughes, J. (2004) Family Wealth – Keeping it in the Family. Bloomberg Press.

Hughes asserts that to create a genuinely flourishing family, one must also focus on building the family's human, Intellectual, Social, and Spiritual capital and use the family's financial resources to create all these forms of capital. These four types of capital are discussed in detail in the chapter by Mary Duke and Stacy Allred.

Building on this idea, I would assert that a family can't truly build a sense of emotional ownership or a sense of family emotional and business emotional cohesion without investing in growing their human, intellectual, social, and spiritual capital.

To survive and thrive across generations, a family office must put the family's purpose, meaning, and development at its center. This means that the family office needs to see a central part of its purpose as fostering a sense of connection and unity among the family and a sense of pride and identity in what the family is doing (by engaging in investing, philanthropy, growing businesses, and helping family members realize their potential).

Cultivating and acting on purpose creates a sense of connection among the family and motivates people to want to be responsible and engaged stewards rather than passive clients. Building on ideas and questions offered by Björnberg and Nicholson, we offer a few questions that can help you assess the level of emotional ownership in your family:

- Does our family identify with the family office? Do they feel it is aligned with their values and beliefs?

- Do family members feel close to the family office? Do they know and care about the people and what it is trying to accomplish?

- Does what happens to the family office matter to the family? Is continuity important?

- Does the family office give family members a sense of identity? Are they proud of the office and what it is doing?

## Stepping up to the Challenge: Creating a Transformative Family Office

When we talk about putting meaning and purpose at the center of the family office, we are talking about a fundamental shift in how we think about structure and staff family offices. We are fighting generations of thinking about the stated needs of the family and moving to identifying and working on the actual needs of the family. But, in doing so, we offer the opportunity for the family to tap into something much more profound and long-lasting. We are offering the opportunity to create a transformative family office.

## What is a Transformative Family Office?

A transformative family office cultivates a sense of unity and purpose among a family about who they are, what their values are, and the impact that they want to have in the world. They see their financial capital as not just something they grow and protect. They see their financial capital as a resource to invest in the growth of their human, social, intellectual, and spiritual capital. Through holistic management of all their types of capital, they create an impact that enriches the family and impacts the people, businesses, and communities they engage with. They make the world a better place.

## How Do We Build the Transformative Family Office?

Building a foundation for the family office that will generate a sense of emotional ownership to sustain the office over the long term requires the family to put a sense of purpose and meaning at the center of the family office. The protection, growth, and deployment of financial capital should serve that purpose. The family will need to work with the family office team and outside guides to cultivate this sense of purpose and emotional ownership. It will require the time and engagement of the family and the family office team: an ongoing practice.

**Building a holistic leadership model for the family office**. The traditional staffing and structure of a family office aren't sufficient to fulfill the promise of a transformative family office. Creating the transformative family office will require that leadership of the family office is structured so that the family office has the skill sets needed to fulfill a transformative purpose. To do so, the transformative family office needs to diversify the knowledge base of the leadership team and see family cohesion as a central goal for the leadership team. I would suggest that the leadership team include the following:

**A Chief Family Cohesion Officer**. One individual is tasked with working with internal and external resources to ensure a unified and connected family ownership group. Someone charged with creating a mindset within the family that Pieper & Astrachan describe as "Favoring preservation and collective service over consumption and individual, self-serving behavior." Create a reason for being for the family office beyond just growing the financial capital.

**A Chief Learning Officer.** An individual dedicated to investing in and building the human capital of the family and the family office team.

**Training.** All Family Office staff are involved in and committed to learning about the human side of the family office.

If a family office doesn't have the size and complexity to warrant the hiring of these positions, these functions should be assigned to individuals within the organization to focus on.

The transformative family office will need to invest time, money, and energy in the development of the family, family relationships, and family capital. It will also need to develop relationships between the family and the family office team.

## Holistic Goal Setting, Evaluation, and Measurement of Impact

Family offices have become very sophisticated at setting goals and measuring the financial impact of their work. Still, the transformative family office will also need to measure or at least assess the growth and development of human, intellectual, social, and spiritual capital.

Measuring financial success alone won't give a true sense of the long-term health of the family office. In addition, a family must set clear goals aligned with their values in all aspects of the family office. The following are some areas where developing clear goals and objectives can build a true sense of cohesion and connection for the family members to the family office:

**Emotional ownership.** Do family members feel connected to the family office and care about its future and direction? Are they willing to devote time and energy to its long-term success? Are they willing to prepare for and take leadership in the governance roles that help provide vision and direction for the family office?

**Family cohesion.** Is the family cohesive and connected? Can they work through differences effectively and commit to a shared vision? Are they willing to sacrifice for the good of the whole while also recognizing the needs of individual family members? Are they willing to devote time and energy to building their family relationships?

**Philanthropic impact.** Is the family clear about the impact that they want to have as a family with their philanthropic dollars? Is their philanthropy aligned with their family values? Are the systems in place to ensure their philanthropy has the intended impact?

**Community impact.** Are the family members playing meaningful roles in the lives of their communities and society? Are they working to put family values into action to improve the world around us?

**Social impact of investments.** Does the family know about the social impact of the investments that they are making? Are their investment decisions tied to their values? Do they consider the social impact before deploying their capital?

**Individual potential.** Is the family working to help each family member reach their true potential? Are the family and family office working to help family members have a healthy relationship with their wealth? Are family members leading meaningful and fulfilling lives?

**Holistic staffing.** Do we have individuals on the family office team with the talents, skill sets, and passion for helping the family develop emotional ownership and cohesion? Does our team have the capacity to understand complex family dynamics and work with the family to help manage them? Can the team hold healthy boundaries between the family office and team members? Again, this must be an ongoing practice that shapes the culture of the family and family office.

Creating the transformative family office requires us to move beyond looking at just the financial variables in the family office. It requires a commitment to building a sense of purpose, a sense of family cohesion, and a sense of emotional ownership. It requires the family to take on leadership and ensure that the family office has a team that can fulfill its transformative purpose. But the family cannot do this alone. The transformative family office requires effective collaboration between the family and the family office team that serves them.

## Conclusion

The design flaws in the creation of family offices (focus on structure, wealth creation, and the passive deployment of capital) lead to a disconnected and fractured ownership base. Family members are more often a part of the family office because of trust structures and parental decisions rather than their own conscious choice to be a part of this entity. The result is a passive sense of ownership from the family, where the family members see themselves as clients of the family office rather than the owners, threatening the long-term sustainability of not just the family office but also the family relationships.

To create truly sustainable, long-lasting family offices, we must broaden our focus beyond just the family's financial resources. We must look to create a transformative family office that inspires future generations to move beyond being consumers of the services of the family office to emotional ownership of the family office and the impact it can have in the world. An organization that inspires the rising generation to prepare for leadership and take on the responsibilities of creating a vision for their organizations that tap into the family's values to establish a strong sense of purpose that will sustain them for the next generation and beyond.

## Reflection Questions

- What is the current level of family emotional cohesion among the owning family of our family office? Does the family take emotional ownership of the family office and its future?

- Do we have a sense of purpose for our family office that engages all five sources of family capital?

- Can we clearly articulate the impact we as a family wants to have in creating a better world? Through our philanthropy? Through our work in the community?

- Have we considered the social impact our investments make on the world?

- How much time and money are we investing in developing both members of the family and members of the family office team?

- Do we have the skill sets on our leadership or advisory team to build the non-financial capital of the family office?

- Do we have a governance structure that injects transparency, objectivity, and diversity of thought into our planning processes?

---

## The Transformative Family Office: Key Concepts

**Design flaws create a lack of emotional ownership.** The design flaws of the traditional family office can lead to, over time, a passive ownership group who sees the family office from the mindset of a client rather than the view of an owner responsible for the long-term vision, governance, and sustainability of the organization.

**Family purpose at the center of the family office.** To maximize long-term sustainability and address the design flaws, a family office needs to take a transformative view, put the family at the center of the family office, and see the cultivation of family cohesion, meaning, and purpose as a central part of their mission. This means deploying financial capital in pursuit of the family mission and vision and investing in the family's growth, development, and well-being as a central goal.

**A holistic approach to leadership.** The transformative family office takes a holistic approach to leadership of the family office, putting together a team that can manage not only the financial well-being of the family but also look after the growth and development of the family.

**This requires:**

- A leader who understands the importance of family unity and cohesion

- A CCO – A chief cohesion officer – someone tasked with attending to essential family issues and maintaining a cohesive and committed ownership group

- A CLO – Chief Learning Officer – someone tasked with fostering the growth of the individual family members, their understanding of the family office, and the ability of the family to work effectively together.

**Holistic goal setting and evaluation.** To be truly sustainable, the transformative family office needs to set financial goals and goals to develop the family's human, social, and spiritual capital and evaluate progress toward those goals.

**Productive collaboration.** Creating the transformative family office needs to be a productive collaboration between the family and the family office team.

CHAPTER 4

# Family Office Leadership: Investing in the Development of the Professionals

## By Jill Barber and Greg McCann

**When I (Jill Barber) became president of CYMI Holdings** in 2018, I knew we had to continue to evolve the Family Office to remain relevant to the Family, but what did that mean? What steps need to be taken? How would we know if we were successful?

I had worked for CYMI for nearly 20 years. And like most of my colleagues, I was a subject matter expert. If you had an estate planning request, I was your person. If you needed tax help, you would speak to our tax expert. And if you wanted answers about legal matters? You guessed it. You'd talk to our legal expert.

On the surface, this may not sound like a problem. After all, we were masters at putting out fires and had an impressive record of technical accomplishments. But I had to ask the question: Is our current culture the culture that best supports our success today and, more importantly, in the future? We were siloed in our work. Change was incremental, and pivotal conversations occurred in sidebars with select key players—not in team meetings where everyone could participate.

To be sure, we were subject matter experts who were not focused on strategy, teamwork, and vertical leadership development. This created a leadership vacuum with potentially significant consequences in a fast-changing world. As a family office, we could not provide the agile leadership families need for long-term success.

It also meant that our client family—like so many—was ill-positioned to achieve more than the narrow goal of the ongoing accumulation, preservation, and escalation of wealth. As a result, while they made significant investments in philanthropy that led to measurable positive change, much more potential went untapped.

Considering the fact our colleague Jill Shipley addressed in chapter 1—that the inequity between the top 1 percent and the rest of the world is continuing to grow —does this suggest a missed opportunity on a massive scale?

So, as a new president, I turned my focus to how we could change the culture of the family office to develop the capacity of team members throughout the organization so that we were capable not only of mastering technical needs but of providing agile, innovative, relevant, sustainable leadership for the ongoing generations of the family we served.

To help me with this work, I reached out to a longtime family enterprise coach, my co-author of this article, and co-editor of this book, Greg McCann. Over a roughly three-year process, Greg worked with me to help us build the skill sets and capacity we needed.

The single family office, after all, is being redefined. Families' expectations are ever-increasing. And the demands to succeed in more holistic ways in a complex interdependent world require that the family office—especially its leadership—have an ongoing practice to develop its capacity and agility. These qualities are at the heart of the vertical leadership development embraced by the government, business, and nonprofit worlds. For this to happen, the single family office has to be reframed not as a cost center but as an investment to co-create the family's success. The remainder of this chapter explores how we did this at CYMI—and the core ideas you could apply in your own family and family office. Thanks to the Mathile Family and especially our board chair, Mike Mathile, for allowing me to talk openly and honestly about this work.

## The Leadership Triad: Mindset, Capacity, and Agility

Many leadership experts discuss the importance of "horizontal leadership development." They mean developing a team's skills, knowledge, and credentials. And it is, without question, necessary. Without horizontal leadership development, financial, tax, and estate plans will not get accurately done.

But while horizontal leadership development will get these essential tasks done, they do not make true agile leadership possible. That requires vertical leadership development—the stuff of building capacity and agility. In short, both are necessary. But while most family office leaders have invested in their horizontal development, there has been relatively little investment in vertical leadership to date. From our view, it is a great missing link.

So, what is involved in vertical leadership development? Fundamentally, it rests on these three core ideas: The Family Enterprise Mindset, Capacity, and Agility.

## The Family Enterprise Mindset

When you cultivate a family enterprise mindset, it means that your family office team and the client family recognize the family enterprise as one that is organized around the deployment of its finances, talent and relationships into opportunities that align with the family's vision and purpose. It means you have an ongoing practice to make your family's involvement a strategic advantage to all the enterprises in which you are involved. And it means you recognize the need to develop the capacity of everyone in the family enterprise.

In recent years, I (Greg) have had several clients who adopted this mindset as they sold or considered selling their businesses in a way to reframe how they used their wealth. For example, one family created a new position of Chief Learning Officer and named a family member to it. They also shifted their investments to better align with their values. They initiated a multi-million-dollar collective family philanthropic effort that the family also led. And they only used part-time outside investment advisors, which shows both the shift away from nonfamily and the relative decline in the importance of investing.

Since families are increasingly involved in multiple industries, and the industries they are involved with are changing rapidly, the enduring aspect of family enterprises is often the family. To cope with and capitalize on this rate of change requires a proactive investment in developing the capacity and agility of both the family and its enterprises. This may be especially applicable in the single family office, where the family often falls short in its ownership. For more on a comparison of the mindset of running a family business with that of a single family office, see the Perceptions and Actions Chart in the Wealth: Perception Shapes Reality chapter.

## Capacity

The second element of the vertical leadership triad focuses on developing the capacity of family members and/or family office members to be more self-aware, empathetic, and able to frame complex issues effectively.

It reflects the ability to step back from a situation (be it your ego, family, industry, or culture) and see and experience things more insightfully. This is not about acquiring more skills but about *transforming* the leader.

For example, I (Jill) recall when a family member came to me concerned about their strategy for their estate plan. The conversation revolved around the technical instructions for distributions. As we talked, I sensed that the technical instructions were not the real issue and continued to reframe the problem for the client. Eventually, they realized they wanted to ensure their children understood the "why" behind the distribution language and were anxious about how to have the conversation. We devised a fireside chat, which could be recorded, to share insights into their thought process.

If I had solved the initial problem, the distribution language in the agreement would be different. But the issue and the anxiety would still exist. By slowing down, reframing the problem, and being empathic to the emotionality of the issue, we got to a solution that solved the real problem.

There are many ways to develop one's capacity, and no one approach is inherently better.

But some are better suited to the person or family and their goals. Through the leadership agility model we use, some avenues include:

- Working with a coach.

- Seeking out and giving more feedback.

- Putting yourself in new environments that expose you to new people and new thinking.

- Creating stretch goals.

- Meditation.

- Creating "white space," or a time to reflect, process, and create: something the majority of people at the most evolved stages of leadership have as a daily practice.

Let's dive into this critical element a bit more deeply. To paraphrase Frederic Laloux's work in *Reinventing Organizations*: An organization can't evolve beyond the capacity of its leaders.[26] So, I worked with Greg for several months to understand and apply these concepts, reframe the issues at CYMI, and determine our best path to bringing these concepts and skills to my leadership team.

After that, we held a meeting with the leadership team to get everything on the table and bring them further into the discussion. That led to a two-day offsite and numerous Zoom meetings with Greg to immerse ourselves in applying these concepts. We then intentionally brought these practices into our weekly leadership team meetings and virtually every other meeting we held.

The rest of the staff saw the changes in how we showed up and asked to be included in the work. We led by example. We made mistakes and owned them, and we did that in front of the staff. We empathized with our team members and apologized when we fell back into our old patterns.

Today we continue to work on validating others when they show that agility and capacity. This work is work—it is an ongoing practice—in every interaction, every meeting, every day.

This work came to life—across my team—when we were presented with an investment opportunity to purchase a single-tenant building. In the past, we would have covered all the bases from a technical perspective. That was still the case in this transaction. But there was added emphasis in two areas: the impact on the family system and the collaboration within CYMI.

---

[26] Laloux, F. (2015). Reinventing organizations: ein Leitfaden zur Gestaltung sinnstiftender Formen der Zusammenarbeit. Vahlen.

Members of the leadership team worked together, with me intentionally leaning back and trusting the rest of my Leadership Team to handle it, to bring a group together to brainstorm the options for this transaction—including how this transaction could model how CYMI could support the family into the future. The team also explored what investing together for future generations might look like, how to create investment vehicles that balanced independence with interdependence, and how to create a win for all generations and a win for CYMI. They devised a strategy that created those wins, and the family recognized and appreciated the work that went into getting to the favorable outcome.

The pinnacle was when the family members began commenting on the shift in the team and that we seemed more connected and working more collaboratively. Leadership skills were built and utilized at every level in an organization. The family and our staff saw the changes from the staff accountant on up.

## Agility

We define agility in leadership as having the mindfulness to decide which style or "gear" best suits the circumstances and goals. Metaphorically, for example, when humans learn to move, we begin with crawling, walking, and perhaps running, riding a bike, and driving a car. Relatively few of us become pilots. And those who do may have the capacity to fly to another country but use their agility to decide that taking a bike to the corner store makes the most sense.

The same is true with leadership. We have to call on different skills at different times. When ordering lunch, you likely will not want to create a working team, brainstorm the options, and ensure everyone is heard and committed to the decision. But when selecting a new fund and general ledger accounting software, those steps would probably make sense and create a better outcome.

As subject matter experts, we tend to move immediately into problem-solving gear. And this is a hard habit to break. There are two ways to help change this habit. First is working on effectively framing the problem, issue, or opportunity, but more about this later. Secondly, at CYMI, to help us develop the new skill, we ask in every meeting, "What gear should we be in?" (See table of what the team at CYMI developed.) This allows the convenor to guide the conversation and pull the group back on topic. It also allows the participant to understand the purpose of the meeting and be prepared as they walk in. The different gears have also given us definitions that everyone understands. What would your family or family office's gears look like?

**Table: What Gear Should We Be In?**

| Feedback | Ratio of 4:1—four positive comments for every critical comment. Give specifics using situation, behavior, and impact. |
| --- | --- |
| Advice/Problem-Solving | Best when asked for and you have experience or expertise. This is what many of us are prone to give automatically. |
| Support / Validation | Validate what the other person is feeling. It is not fixing or changing anything. |
| Peer | Can I ask the other person for help? |
| Coaching | Trust the other person has the answer you are helping them discover it. |

| Brainstorming | Think without constraints or criticism or need to connect all the dots. |
| --- | --- |
| Reverse | I messed up. Can we "reverse" and start the conversation again? |

## A Closer Look: The Leadership Agility Model Applied

The overarching model for the work we did at CYMI was adapted from *Leadership Agility* by Bill Joiner and Stephen Josephs.[27] It is based on studying 800 leaders, looking at the stages they evolve through relative to important or pivotal conversations, teamwork, and leading organizational change. It provides a roadmap for leadership development. The concept is that leaders develop four fundamental agilities so that they have greater depth, are more accessible in (or closer to) the present moment and integrate with the other agilities.

Self-awareness is self-explanatory. At CYMI, this included coaching, the Myers-Briggs Type Indicator, increased feedback, and even some meditation.

The second agility is empathy, which is tied into the vulnerability-based trust work we did as the foundation of the Five Behaviors of a Cohesive Team (discussed below).

The third agility, the one most often overlooked, is framing.

[27] Joiner, B., & Josephs, S. (2007). Leadership agility: Five levels of mastery for anticipating and initiating change. Reflections: The SoL Journal, 8(1), 44-51.

Framing is stepping back before problem-solving and assessing the real issue, problem, or opportunity. In his book, *What's Your Problem?* author Thomas Wedell-Wedellsborg cites a survey of CEOs of organizations in seventeen countries, and 85 percent said their organizations were poor at framing.[28] They jump too quickly into problem-solving. As one client of Greg's says: it is so seductive just to get stuff done! Most of our (Jill and Greg's) coaching conversations revolve around effective framing.

The fourth agility is innovation, creating value from change. CYMI has done a great job at adopting the innovative practices of the industry, such as the internally managed investment portfolio, the CYMI Private Capital Services, and the Thing 1 staff development program (which is all about developing the whole person).

## Leadership Agility and Levels

Though we all vary in what stage or level we are at any given moment, we tend to have a home base. There are five relevant stages. Here is a quick look, followed by a discussion about the various stages.

---

[28] Wedell-Wedellsborg, T. (2017). Are you solving the right problems. Harvard Business Review, 95(1), 76-83.

**Table: Leadership Agility Model**

| Level of Agility | Mindset | Pivotal Conversations | Teamwork | Organizational Change (Culture) |
|---|---|---|---|---|
| **Synergist** (~1%) | Holistic aligns their purpose with benefitting others. Leadership is a path to personal transformation. | Fully integrated in use of accommodating and advocating. Highly present, empathetic, and deeply connected with others, even in difficult conversations. | Extremely agile in bringing the most effective leadership approach to benefit the team bring about the best results for the team and individuals on it. | Highly aware of each stakeholder's needs, perspectives, and goals. Able to achieve ideal results even from seemingly unsolvable conflicts or opposing goals. |
| **Co-Creator** (~4%) | Cultivates a shared purpose and vision. Driven by service to others. | Open to, and grounded when receiving (even negative) feedback. Highly agile balancing accommodating and advocating styles. | Develops collaborative teams who feel responsibility for the overall organization. Agile in leadership style but prefers a consensus approach. | Develops collaborative stakeholder relationships that focus on the common good with awareness of societal impact. |

| | | | | |
|---|---|---|---|---|
| **Catalyst** (~5%) | Visionary: "It's not about me", Leading not doing. | Assertive & accommodative, genuinely care about input. | Facilitator, open exchange in conversations,the team and individuals on it. | Creates participative culture, empowers direct reports. |
| **Acheiver** (~35%) | Strategic outcome, leading more. | Assertive, accept and initiate feedback. | Gain buy-in from team and think strategically. | Strategies to gain stakeholder gains, analysis of industry. |
| **Expert** (~45%) | Always busy doing, but exhausted. | Lead when absolutely needed and one way. | Individual contributor. | Company focused and tactical. |

Source: Adapted from Leadership Agility by Joiner & Josephs.

Approximately 45 percent of leaders have the expert stage as their homebase, 35 percent have the achiever, and 10 percent evolve to the catalyst stage or beyond. At the expert level, self-awareness, empathy, framing, and innovation are less developed, integrated, and available. There is a tendency to frame things as a problem that the expert is responsible for solving. (For example, "I will fire Fred because he is underperforming.") At this level, your identity is closely tied to being the one to solve the problem or the *hero*, as termed in the model.

The achiever's agilities are more evolved and more integrated, and there is additional capacity to step back and see the system and think more strategically when necessary (maybe Fred isn't the problem, but our training *system* is.) At this level, there is still that sense of being the problem solver or hero, but a growing capacity to seek input and buy-in.

At the catalyst level, the agilities are integrated and available at the moment. At this level, the additional capacity to see and shape the culture emerges. A significant shift happens—you are no longer attached to being the hero. It is a gear you can access but one you can also shift out of.

At the synergist and co-creator stages, which comprise about 5 percent of leaders studied, there is the capacity to see and create new organizations, think more globally, and create more breakthrough innovation, with ever-deeper awareness, in the present moment.

It is worth noting that at each stage of this development, you still retain the capacities of the early stages. I (Jill) have been assessed to have the capacity at the co-creator level, yet still can downshift, when necessary (mindfully) or when under stress (unintentionally), to the expert approach of typically framing things as a problem that they must solve.

## A Leadership Agility Mini-Case Study from Another SFO

A CEO of a single family office (who had also worked with Greg) was a participant at the Gathering and who has led similar efforts in the single family office she leads, shared a poignant example of how the development work in her family office has powerfully influenced her client family. In collaboration with the family, she has added to her annual evaluation the following questions:

How does the Family Office contribute to:

- Your health and happiness?

- A sense of meaning and purpose?

- Alignment of values and easier decision-making as a family?

- Engagement of the next generation?

This demonstrates self-awareness of her role, empathy for what the family wants, framing her role and its value more effectively, and innovating how her role and implicitly the role of the entire family office is defined. Indeed, catalyst-level leadership, if not higher!

## The Five Behaviors of a Cohesive Team

CYMI's work also involved using The Five Behaviors of a Cohesive Team, developed by Patrick Lencioni at The Table Group.[29] This

---

[29] Lencioni, P. (2012). The five dysfunctions of a team. Pfeiffer, a Wiley Imprint, San Francisco.

model integrates into the Leadership Agility work quite effectively. The work on this allows the team to benchmark against The Table Group's database of over 13,000 participants in The Five Behaviors Program. The progress the CYMI leadership team made was impressive. (This is based on a self-reported assessment through The Table Group at Wiley benchmarked against a database of other teams. See the table below, which lists the five behaviors.)

|  | 2020 | 2021 |
|---|---|---|
| **Vulnerability-based Trust** | 54% | 93% |
| **Conflict** | 32% | 86% |
| **Commitment** | 14% | 71% |
| **Accountability** | 49% | 90% |
| **Results** | 44% | 52% |

## The Results and Impact

In my (Greg's) years of working with teams, I have observed Jill and her leadership team made a more concerted effort to apply this work daily than any team I have worked with on this model. I did one-on-one sessions with each leadership team member. Each team member was asked to champion one of the five behaviors. They worked to bring it into their daily work, including one-on-one interactions, leadership team meetings, and staff meetings. They were also open to individual coaching; some used peer networks and intermittent coaching.

We've framed the results in terms of three leadership agility areas: pivotal conversations, teamwork, and organizational change and culture—since the goal was to accelerate the team's capacity and agility in each of these domains.

## Pivotal Conversations

In the beginning, the family office culture was such that conflict and feedback were often avoided. Often the meeting was happening outside of or after the meeting. Also, people weren't getting feedback on what they were doing right or what they could improve on. Through this work, the leadership team and, to a lesser extent, the entire staff are engaging in productive conflict.

The Leadership Team was working on prioritizing the workload for the year. Each member had biases toward what was important to accomplish based on their perspective. There was a debate on each item brought to the table, but no one left. No one acquiesced and then harbored resentment after the meeting. Everyone stayed at the table, and we worked with the differences in opinions. All felt heard and could commit to the year's priorities. The meeting happened in and during the meeting.

## Teamwork

The leadership team transformed individually and collectively. I (Jill) crafted an invitation to people who were candidates for the leadership team with expectations, roles, and responsibilities. It was OK to decline this invitation, which one candidate did. As a result, the team developed into a more cohesive and effective team, and as most members of the team led a team, they were able to improve their teams as well.

The Investment Team has an important job in our office—the markets move quickly, and there is a high level of focus on their expertise that has a real dollar impact on the Family and the Family Office if not attended to. With that said, led by the CIO, the team has stepped into this work and instigated conversations with the Wealth Advisory Team to see how they could assist them in communicating complex investment concepts to the Family members. The Investment Team has also worked with our Private Capital Team to make available online research tools that can help in their analysis and decision making—all which takes time away from the portfolio. Still, they see that it adds value to the entire system.

## Organizational Change and Culture

Building vulnerability-based trust within the organization is the foundation of the five behaviors and the start of much of the evolution of the culture. In March of 2022, we held an all-staff workshop that Greg and I co-created. One of our key goals was to empower the leadership team members to focus on developing their leadership and teamwork skills. We even co-created challenges each team faced and asked them to consider approaching them from a catalyst level. The teams met individually to focus on their respective issues, then we gathered, under Greg's facilitation and coaching, to learn the outcomes of each group's work.

When the investment team spoke, they showed a willingness (with some coaching) to go to a deeper, more vulnerable level than others. Led by the investment relationship manager, they said that they felt a huge responsibility to keep CYMI and the Family flush with capital.

But at the same time, they did not always feel like they fit into the organization and did not understand the disconnect.

The rest of the organization was stunned. In one poignant moment, someone from another team said, almost to himself: "I bet that is how all of us feel." And many others began to empathize with and validate the issue. As I (Jill) listened, I felt grateful that this issue that had been unspoken for many years was now out in the open, thanks to the investment team's willingness to be vulnerable.

Since then, there has been a palpable shift in the culture of our organization to be more aware of inclusion and validation. While we still have a long way to go, at least we are on the path. To us, this clearly illustrates the fact that the leader needs to own that she can influence and shape the culture. Most family offices we see have their culture influenced by the family's culture without even knowing it. We politely challenge family office leaders to develop their culture so we can have a positive influence on the families!

## Conclusion

Recently, I (Jill) was sitting at a conference dealing with trends with SFOs and noticed I was *actually present*. Because of our work to cultivate the team's capacity and agility, I wasn't on my device putting out fires, solving an endless stream of problems, and feeling like Indiana Jones running ahead of that boulder. In this partnership with the client family, we see the vital need for the family office to do its part to cultivate an ongoing practice to develop the leadership capacity and agility of everyone.

Analogous to working out, doing this involves some sweating, heavy lifting, and stretching. Still, it leads to a greater ability to be present, to have the white space needed to lead and innovate, and be far more effective in leading change. Just as no one advocates waiting to work out until you have had your first heart attack. Doing this work also helps you make far better choices to avoid a crisis, capitalize on opportunities, and transform as individuals and a team.

Every leader we know wants white space—more time to invest in deep thinking without distraction to grapple with the dramatic change, complexity, and interdependencies unique to SFOs.

Without that investment, too much potential is lost. That white space isn't just a result of good leadership but also a cause. Ultimately, this process creates value for the family office staff, and the family in all types of capital.

## Reflection Questions and Rationales

### Rate yourself on a scale of 1-5 with 1 being Definitely Yes and 5 being Definitely No

1.  **Are you a leader or striving to become one?**

    It sounds simplistic but true. If you want to know if you are leading, see if anyone is following you. Leadership is not a title or a position but rather an ability to set a vision, gain alignment or buy-in from key people, and commit resources. You can lead in your family, its enterprises, its philanthropy, or anywhere in your life. "Do you want to lead?" is the question.

2.  **Do you want a safe, neutral place to process ideas, challenges, and opportunities?**

    This is a precious resource. Especially in the overlapping, complex, and interdependent roles of a family enterprise, it is as difficult as it is valuable to have someone who can listen to you say something such as "I feel inadequate for this new challenge," and not have them (your employees, for example) become anxious, try to immediately reassure you (such as your spouse), or fix it (most people default to this approach whenever stress arises). Do you want someone objective who can help you explore the challenge, dig deeper to see if it is a pattern, help you analyze if you have options you haven't considered, or even help you reframe your perspective?

3.  **Do you want someone to guide you to your truth rather than tell you what to do?**

    A leadership coach is not, as many assume, like an athletic coach from school who tells you what to do. A coach trusts the answer and helps explore your patterns, assumptions, and perspectives so that you gain insight into who you are and how you might move toward success as you define it. Are you ready to take greater ownership of your career and, ultimately, your life?

4.  **Are you courageous and willing to be challenged and vulnerable to build on your strengths and work on your shortcomings?**

    Coaching is working on the thing you can most change: yourself. A counterintuitive truth I have found in coaching (and consulting) is that virtually every breakthrough with a client arises when they get vulnerable. A truth arises. At the same time, most people struggle far more to own their strengths than their weaknesses, so you can lean into achieving your potential. Do you want to truly own your strengths and learn to better navigate your weaknesses? "All of humanity's problems stem from man's inability to sit quietly in a room alone." — Blaise Pascal, Pensées

5.  **Do you value and seek out objective feedback?**

    According to the Center for Creative Leadership, the number one risk to derail your career as you move up in an organization is a lack of *objective* feedback. I believe there is an even greater risk in a family enterprise where conflict is so often avoided. All good leaders seek out feedback from others and are generous with giving feedback. Do you want to hear from those you are leading? Do you want to offer them the same gift?

6.  **Do you want to work on your career and life, not just in it?**

    If your life feels like Indiana Jones running ahead of that boulder, you may gain some satisfaction from striving, suffering, and feeling stress, but it takes a toll on you, your business, and your life. As one client of Greg's says: "We don't reward suffering, just performance." Are you ready to work *on* your life and career?

7.  **Do you want more white space to think and process deeply?**

    Every one of my clients holds the goal of creating white space (that is, time and space for deep thinking) as a priority. If you are a leader trying to change a system, it is vital. Are you creating enough white space for what you and your family enterprise need?

Are you willing to let go of an attachment to feeling busy being a measure of your importance or worth?

8. **There are predictable stages leaders evolve through. Do you know where you are now and where you want to be?**

   Few people can articulate what a good leader is and therefore struggle to see where they want to evolve as a leader. Do you want a roadmap for where you are, where you want to be, and how to get there?

9. **Is self-care a priority for you?**

   If these recent years taught us anything, we must take care of ourselves, body, mind, and soul. The tank must get refilled. Would being accountable to a coach help you with this?

10. **Can you define what success looks like for you?**

    You, not the coach, must answer this. For example, the year I (Greg) retired from 27 years in academia, I sought a coach with one primary goal: to not fill up all that time with work. I am proud to share that success was achieved! Though it can and should evolve, can you articulate what success looks like for your career and life?

- If your score is 26 (or higher), you may want to wait, reflect, and check back in 3-6 months.
- If 15-25, at least take the next step and set up a call to explore things with a coach.
- If under 15, what are you waiting for?

Excerpt from *Assessing Your Readiness for a (Family Enterprise) Leadership Coach* by Greg McCann. Source: Wealth of Wisdom: Top Practices for Wealthy Families and Their Advisors; Tom McCullough and Keith Whitaker; Copyright © 2022 Tom McCullough and Keith Whitaker. Adapted with permission of John Wiley & Sons, Inc."

CHAPTER

# 5

# The Role of Learning in the Family-Centered Office: A Pathway to Building Capacities Needed to Thrive

## By Stacy Allred and Mary Duke[30]

**If the family isn't flourishing,** how important is their financial wealth?

In today's fast-changing environment, if you aren't learning, you aren't just standing still, you are going backward. In this ever more complex and rapidly changing 21st century, learning and adapting are critical superpowers! A family can create a brilliant network of sophisticated estate planning and money management structures, but to thrive, the family members need to develop the capacity to learn, understand and integrate the complexity and interdependencies of their families and the world in which they live.

While economists differ on what label to use for it,[31] they broadly

---

[30] Credit to Scott Peppet for the term "Family-Centered Office."

[31] The 21st century has been called the Intangible Economy, the Fourth Economy, the Entrepreneurial Economy, etc.

agree the world is entering a new economy characterized by unprecedented change, extraordinary complexity, and unpredictable challenges.

This creates a crucible of change for families and the family offices (FO) that serve them. New challenges arise daily. Equipping a family to address new challenges, and even more, to find ways to leverage these very challenges as opportunities, is something family offices should be adept at. Not many are. And it is up to the family itself to drive the shift in culture and priorities in their family office if they are looking to unlock this potential.

*Meet the Ballard family (name changed), currently in its fifth to seventh generations. The family's leadership recently attended a retreat with other legacy families, and their interest was piqued by the idea of growing a great family.*

*As part of our onboarding interviews, we met with their family office team, who described the very sophisticated family enterprise system they oversaw on behalf of the family. It includes a well-staffed family office team of highly experienced subject matter experts, a private trust company with sophisticated investment capabilities overseeing both traditional and alternative portfolios, and an impressive operating company and real estate empire—both with global scope. They have leveraged remarkable technology to provide aggregated reporting and transaction processing, monitor IT security, and model sophisticated tax planning strategies. They are incredibly buttoned down as family offices go!*

*But interestingly, when asked about the family members and how they were doing, the family office off-handedly noted that each member of the rising gen was provided with a briefing on their 18th birthday and sent to a "wildly popular next-gen training program" put on in various exotic locations by one of their private banks. Other than simply pumping out cash and the odd special distribution for purchasing cars and homes, there was little, if any, awareness of how the family members were doing in terms of flourishing. This was borne out by the absence of airtime allocated on meeting agendas or calendars and the lack of staffing or consultants skilled in (and dedicated to) growing the capacity and well-being of family members. On further discussion, it became clear the family office had a somewhat fixed view of the individuals in the family, based primarily on anecdotes repeatedly replayed among the staff. It felt as if the family was seen as a bit of an impediment to the great work the FO team was doing: the incredible sophistication and effectiveness of the tax and estate plan, the remarkable returns of their carefully curated investments in highly selective private deals, and the well-oiled property, yacht, and aircraft management system they had in place.*

*The Ballard's new intention of growing their family's qualitative capital presents a significant opportunity, a 'moment that matters' with an outsized impact on the family and the family office who support them to lean into creating an intentional, lifelong journey of growing human capital. How might the Ballards move from awareness to action?*

## Design

There are design flaws in typical FOs that impede the ability to adapt to this new world. Let's consider the common origin story of a family office. A family office does not appear out of the mist but typically evolves out of a wealth creator's existing support system. Often the financial, legal, and/or tax advisors who were involved with the recent **IPO** or helped develop the company credit facilities or managed the books and records are trusted and simply brought along as the founder's needs grow more complex. These fledgling service platforms generally have little to do with family; they primarily focus on supporting the founder.

As the founder's needs and actual family grow, the services evolve to support the complex administrative and compliance requirements of the various structures that are the natural byproducts of financial wealth, namely trusts, partnerships, and holding companies. It is only later that the services evolve to be a true family office—one that is focused on the growth and flourishing of each family member and the family system over generations. This flags up the first design flaw.

## SFOs are Largely Staffed by Technical Specialists Who Focus on Money

Money is easy to measure and is the yardstick by which society measures economic wealth. There are entire armies of professionals minted every year who are equipped to help manage money and the attendant details—such as the trusts, holding companies, investment portfolios, and direct investments. These technicians have highly specialized knowledge with CVs sprinkled with the familiar MBA, LLM, JD, CPA, CFP, etc. These highly technical fields tap into a numerate, logical, and left-brain mindset. (Admittedly, both authors come with this bias, as our training was anchored in these specialized fields.)

James (Jay) E. Hughes, Jr. first raised the issue in his 1991 book *Family Wealth: Keeping it in the Family*.[32] He challenges us to consider the family's balance sheet and recognize that its most significant asset is the family itself: its members and their relations, works, and contribu-

---

[32] Hughes Jr, J. E. (2010). Family Wealth: Keeping It in the Family--How Family Members and Their Advisers Preserve Human, Intellectual, and Financial Assets for Generations. John Wiley & Sons.

tions. Who among this alphabet soup of family office professionals is equipped to assess and help grow the critical asset of family members?

This chapter builds on the foundational ideas of Jay, our dear friend and mentor, whose fingerprints are throughout as we, along with other early adopters in the field,[33] vigorously strive to put the ideas of growing the family's intangible capital into practice, making it a reality.

The saying goes, "You get what you measure!" Money is easy to measure and easy to track. It is relatively simple to see whether it has grown or declined. The same cannot be said for the intangible capital of a family—its people. But we would caution that just because money is easy to measure, it does not mean it is the only asset worthy of attention. Douglas Hubbard's *How to Measure Anything* posits that if a thing can be observed, it lends itself to measurement. No matter how "fuzzy" the measure is, it's still a measurement if it tells you more than you knew before.[34]

This brings us to our next design flaw.

## Not Enough Diversity of Thought

Family offices, by nature, are small, protective teams formed to support the views and decisions of a wealth creator. This provides a perfect

[33] Scott, Peppet, (2021) Family-Focused Office, published by Family Firm Institute.

[34] "For a deeper dive into creating your own measurement practice, see Measurement Demystified: Creating Your L&D Measurement, Analytics, and Reporting Strategy, David Vance and Peggy Parskey (2021), Association for Talent Development Press. (For more on the how to, see also Measurement Demystified Fieldguide.)

crucible for groupthink where the staff tends to cohere around a perceived consensus that most often goes unquestioned.

It is common to find a family office staffed by a group of like-minded advisors—whose similarities can even extend to other attributes they share, like the neighborhood where they live, religion, schools, clubs, and even the cars they drive.

And all these like-minded people often have another critical trait in common: risk aversion. Attorneys and accountants primarily focus on minimizing exposure to risk and limiting the potential for losses and lawsuits. Even the investment specialists in a family office tend to have a bias toward loss avoidance (preservation mindset). This insular and defensive team may present a barrier to the open, creative, and diverse thought that can ideate new approaches to confront and capitalize on the rapidly changing world in which we live. What is the natural outcome? It undermines innovation.

But wait, there's more! This tendency toward team insularity and risk aversion is compounded by the very nature of the family they serve. A family typically shares both genetics and the social-emotional environment of the members' upbringing. Further, the insulating impact of financial wealth can buffer the family from the realities of daily life and the challenges confronting those with lesser economic means.

This lack of diversity of thought is something family offices need

---

[35] "For a deeper dive into creating your own measurement practice, see Measurement Demystified: Creating Your L&D Measurement, Analytics, and Reporting Strategy, David Vance and Peggy Parskey (2021), Association for Talent Development Press. (For more on the how to, see also Measurement Demystified Fieldguide.)

to work actively to overcome. We will address ways a family can be very intentional in its efforts to break out of its isolation and be exposed to new and different ideas, approaches, and innovations. Warren Buffet actively seeks diversity of thought by inviting a "credentialed bear" on Berkshire to join a panel of analysts at the annual shareholder meeting that questions Buffet.[36]

## Lack of Mental Agility

A lack of mental agility is a third design flaw that is a barrier to adapting to this new and changing world. This deficit is not unique to family offices or the family members they serve; it cuts across most of society. Mental agility is the ability to think, learn and act upon new information, which is critical to adjust to changing circumstances. And mental agility can be consciously developed and practiced.

This requires the creation of a learning environment, rarely seen in a family office, even though a family office offers an excellent platform for learning. Regrettably, because family offices are too often seen as a cost center, this investment in the future growth and potential of the family is categorized as an expense with a tightly managed budget. It is often referred to as the "soft stuff" and often relegated to some entertainment at a family meeting.

The antidote to these design flaws and the key to navigating this new economy both lie in equipping the family to grow its intangible capital: the family members. This is achieved by implementing a

---

[36] "Wanted: Short Seller to Take on Warren Buffett," Reuters, March 1, 2013.

learning system that touches on every aspect of the family, its enterprise, and its family office. This includes the types of people hired to serve the family, the competencies the office nurtures and rewards, and the priorities it sets and measures its progress against. All of these, taken together, shift the family's culture toward one that is not only ready for change but is equipped to adapt and capitalize on the opportunities that a changing environment presents!

What we are suggesting is no small shift. It requires a sea-change in thinking that starts with the family embracing its growth as an existential priority. Then the family needs to demonstrate to their family office this commitment to invest in growing great family members—not just great investment portfolios! It requires the family and the family office to adopt a mindset that sees its role of growing human capital as equally, if not more important and as impactful as its most brilliant financial investment. Growing its family members is an essential priority of the family office. It is its *raison d'être*, not an expense!

This requires reframing what is often referred to as "the soft stuff" to fully embrace the primacy and importance of focusing on the development of the family.

That means prioritizing, guiding and supporting the family to:

- Work on mission and values.

- Address disruptive family dynamics.

- Build skills to manage naturally arising conflict.

- Navigate generational speed bumps.

In our experience, these are anything but soft matters. They are some of the most complex aspects of serving a family.

Creating a learning system that helps to equip each family member with stage-appropriate skills addresses the number one goal of families: to foster flourishing and combat languishing among the members and across the family collectively. The ripple effect of thriving individuals and thriving families creates a greater impact on thriving communities. Since Aristotle's *Politics*, the family has been seen as the basic building block of society. Strong families and the future citizens they produce make for flourishing societies.

## How to Create a System to Grow a Family's Capital

Somewhat surprisingly, a useful model has emerged in the corporate world. Generally associated with quantitative performance metrics and a laser focus on the bottom line, commercial enterprises have adopted a new focus on their qualitative assets—their employees. Big business has come to recognize that one of their most vital assets is not reflected directly on the balance sheet but instead rides up and down in the elevators each day. It is intangible!

This trend began in the early 1990s when IBM's Jack Welch surprised its Fortune 500 peers by hiring a professor and creating a new C-Suite role, that of the Chief Learning Officer (CLO). More than a re-imagined human resources function, the Chief Learning Officer is focused on growing the developmental capacity of the company's people through learning, leadership development, and performance management. Today, nearly every Fortune 500 firm has a CLO function.[37]

It is worth noting that this trend emerged at the same time a leading authority in the world of family wealth, James E Hughes, Jr., "Jay," challenged our field to look beyond the family's financial capital. He called on us to recognize the extraordinary value and importance of the family itself—placing its members at the top of the family's balance sheet.

This presents the challenge: how to measure or value the family? People do not lend themselves to easy quantifiable measures of value. But that is no reason not to assess and grow them. It simply takes a new framework and some new benchmarks. Fortunately, Jay Hughes provided just such a framework introducing the four forms of intangible capital in a family: human capital, spiritual capital (also called legacy capital), social capital, and intellectual capital.

Just as Modern Portfolio Theory is foundational to investing, these capital concepts are foundational to our work with families and provide the framework a family can utilize in building its learning platform.[38]

## Human Capital

The most fundamental intangible and the most significant asset on the family balance sheet is the family members themselves. Humans are

---

[37] Rowe, Tiffany. "How a Chief Learning Officer Can Take Employee Engagement to the Next Level." Hppy, December 14, 2022. https://gethppy.com/employee-engagement/how-a-chief-learning-officer-can-take-employee-engagement-to-the-next-level

[38] Markowitz, H. (1952). Modern portfolio theory. Journal of Finance, 7(11), 77-91.

far more precious than money and are irreplaceable.

How do we assess and grow the flourishing of family members? The ancient Greeks defined happiness as the innate sense of moving toward one's potential. We are essentially looking at the actualization of individuals, and Maslow gives us a helpful baseline hierarchy for considering this. His framework recognizes that an individual can only progress to higher functioning if foundational needs have been satisfied. Humans start with physiological needs such as food and clothing. Once these are secured, personal safety, which in our society most often presents as economic security, can be addressed. After safety is achieved, love and belonging become the priority as the quest for meaningful relationships emerges. Then esteem and self-actualization enter the frame, capped by transcendence. Suppose any one of the more basic needs is suddenly unmet—for example, an unexpected job loss. In that case, the shift will cause a setback that lowers the individual's focus on the quest for personal security.

Numerous assessments and interviewing approaches can help gauge how family members are doing on this journey of actualization. They typically look at the individual's happiness, life satisfaction, meaning and purpose, values, character and virtue, close social relationships, and mental and physical health.[39] But assessing and growing human capital requires more than administering an assessment and reviewing the results.

There is widespread misunderstanding of assessments in family

---

[39] To learn more, see Positive Psychology Center at the University of Pennsylvania, including Dr. Martin (Marty) Seligman's PERMATM and the theory of well-being.

offices. Too often, they are used as entertainment to add a bit of fun or "soft stuff" to a family meeting. Family members take an assessment, and a bit of time is spent reviewing the results. There are usually a few "a-ha" moments of new self-awareness or insights into why there are strains in relationships, but this is the end of the discussion too often. Frequently, the assessment reports are tucked away in desk drawers, and the opportunity for development through truly integrating the learning is lost. Assessments should be used as the first step on a journey of personal growth. The heavy lifting begins with transforming new awareness into action through shifting mindsets, adopting new behaviors, and building these behaviors into habits. This takes practice over time and is best affected by the support of a coaching relationship.

Assessing and growing human capital involves highly qualitative attributes that require special skills to assess and understand. Physical as well as psychological well-being should also be included.[40] These skills are rarely found in a typical family office's highly technical subject-matter experts.

Families that embrace the priority of growing human capital are prioritizing it in their family offices, where they are adding human developmental expertise to their teams, either by hiring senior professionals or engaging them on retainer. Doing this requires the family and their family office executives to prioritize this work and see it as a critical investment, not an expense.

Investing in the family's human capital is vital because the progress

---

[40] An example of the progress to measure well-being is The World Well-Being Project (WWBP). See wwbp.org to understand how they are pioneering scientific techniques for measuring psychological well-being and physical health based on the analysis of social media.

of each individual helps increase the functioning. The developmental growth of even one family member positively impacts the family system. And well-functioning family systems are the very foundation of our society. Additionally, a well-functioning family with significant financial resources has the capacity to both see their responsibility to society and act on it.

*Over two years, through a series of one-on-one and couple's interviews, assessments, and surveys, the Ballard family began to understand better who they are, individually and collectively, and where they are starting their developmental journey. The family engaged a leadership development firm with experience coaching families with owned enterprises to administer some assessments and to pair off with family members in personal coaching relationships. This is where the heavy lifting of internalizing the insights gleaned from assessments and interviews takes place, and new behaviors can be adopted and practiced into a habit. The family is looking forward to re-taking these assessments in the coming months to see where they have made progress and what new growth areas are identified.*

*In addition, the family worked with the family office to ensure the performance management system included metrics for the entire family office team to have measurements of their contributions to growing the intangible capital of the family. The family asked that a balance sheet be designed to reflect their human capital and that the subject be added as a standing item on their meeting agendas. They set aside a significant budget to support this investment in their family and the family office team. This would now be a priority for everyone.*

## Spiritual Capital

Having spiritual capital means a family has a purpose that is bigger than simply enjoying the accouterments of great financial capital. It involves a family sharing and sustaining an intention that transcends individual interests. It does not require a religious context, although it is often connected with a family's faith tradition. This starts with embracing a holistic understanding that wealth is not money, but well-being, in all its forms.

A family with spiritual capital has examined its individual and collective perceptions of this more significant meaning of wealth. An understanding of how the family perceives the purpose of its wealth and the vision they have for using it in the world are the foundations of spiritual capital.

A fundamental humility is required to nurture a family's spiritual capital because it requires a family to recognize its connections to each other and the greater world. A family with high spiritual capital understands the power in the relationships between each member and knows that together the family is better equipped to navigate the challenges ahead. This appreciation fosters deep gratitude—another aspect of a family's spiritual capital.

Each generation must decide what their family and its true wealth mean. Families cannot sustain being held together by edict, force, or even the economic ties of financial wealth. On reaching adulthood, each member must examine the social contract they make to give up some personal freedom to be part of the family system. And having considered the exchange, they must see the benefit they derive. And importantly, the decision to remain is not to either stay or go. As part of growing into adulthood, each member can decide how and when to be part of the family group.

Understanding spiritual capital requires an understanding of the fundamental polarity in families that exists between love and power. The pull of love is the primal force calling for togetherness and survival. But love sits in eternal tension with power and its clarion call to autonomy, the lure to strike out and seek independence.

Polarities are never resolved. Instead, they must be managed in a way that involves constantly balancing the push and pull of love and power over time.[41]

Family offices must be ready to help a family consider these existential questions—first individually and then for the family. This requires the family and its office to overcome the design flaw of a lack of diversity of thinking, allowing space for differing opinions, flexibility in ways of engaging, and openness to new ways of being together. And it requires competencies well outside of highly technical staffing in the traditional family office model.

*Using their annual family retreat as a launch pad, the Ballard family started redefining their purpose as a family. This involved some initial work to understand each individual's values and how these came together for the whole. It required the family members to examine their relationship with financial wealth and work on exploring ways they might reframe the way they see their role with each other in the community and the world.*

---

[41] Navigating Polarities: Using Both/And Thinking to Lead Transformation, Brian Emerson and Kelly Lewis, Paradoxical Press, 2019.

*This also involved some courageous, mediated conversations addressing the family's unspoken hurts and working to build bridges with family members who feel misunderstood or marginalized. This ability to have difficult conversations about known but often undiscussable issues is key to success and sustainability in a family enterprise.*

*The Ballards are still refining their family's mission and working on their vision for the future that can accommodate their different perspectives, diverse goals, and time available to invest in family togetherness. This work on their spiritual capital is not "done in a day." It is an ongoing exploration worthy of the time and attention of the family.*

## Social Capital

A family's social capital is measured in its ability to function effectively. There is no better measure of a family's functioning than its ability to make difficult decisions under pressure together. This shared decision-making system does not come easily or naturally in a family. This need can be made jarringly clear for the generations living in the immediate shadow of a great wealth creator who typically "calls all their own shots," thus providing a very poor role model for shared decisions. How ironic that this same independent soul often saddles future generations with a complex trust and estate structure of joint ownership that requires agile and ongoing collaboration to make decisions.

Another effect of growing up in the wake of a wealth creator is the fear of screwing things up. With such remarkable success in the rearview mirror, the expectation is successes must be huge even to be noticed. Small successes are seen as failures. As a result, family members are inclined to avoid taking any chances that might upset the world order their elders set out. Risk-taking is perceived as anathema. If not combatted, this can result in a cycle of entropy, or decline, of energy that erodes the family's ability to grow.

Families need to be aware of the risk of entropy and take proactive steps to overcome it. An intentional family office can provide a forum for family members to experiment and the learning that comes through unexpected outcomes, sometimes referred to as failures. We like the saying, "FAIL stands for First Attempt Is Learning."

Embracing and rewarding everyone to push outside of comfort, try new things and risk failing is part of the cultural shift in creating a learning focus. This requires a real investment in resources, time, and energy. But consider the costs of failing to grow the family's human capital.

Despite significant advancements in cognitive psychology (the formal name for the field of decision-making), most families rarely use an evidence-based process for thinking through important decisions. Instead, at best, they may tap into the most straightforward tools: the essential pros-and-cons list attributed to Benjamin Franklin. While this may be better than nothing, research over the last 40 years has identified a volume of biases in our thinking that render the pros-and-cons model of decision-making fundamentally flawed. As the Heath brothers advise in their book *Decisive*, "if we aspire to make better choices, then we must learn how these biases work and how to fight them."[42]

---

[42] Heath, C., & Heath, D. (2013). Decisive: How to make better choices in life and work. Random House.

[43] Kross, E., & Grossmann, I. (2012). Boosting wisdom: distance from the self enhances wise reasoning, attitudes, and behavior. Journal of Experimental Psychology: General, 141(1), 43.

Effective decision-making requires us to apply rigor to thinking through a given course of action. It also requires some emotional distance from a problem. Ethan Kross has influential research on 'self-distancing'—viewing a decision or any emotional event from an outside perspective can cool some of the emotions involved in processing things.[43]

But emotions are valuable data (ask: *What is the need behind the emotion?*) and must also be taken into consideration in decisions. Simply ignoring emotions amplifies them. Understanding the emotional component of a decision and balancing the emotional and logical considerations is essential. Other frequent enemies of good decision-making (identified by cognitive psychologists) include starting with an overly narrow set of options, susceptibility to framing effects, overconfidence, and the illusion of control.

Patience and process are key to good group decision-making. A willingness to stick with the messy phase of hearing different ideas, experiences, and perspectives can result in more creativity and emergent ideas, allowing for the co-creation of novel solutions and new thinking needed for this new and complex economy. No one decision-making approach fits all situations, so learning several is essential.

The ability to make timely, collaborative decisions is a generative force in families, and the family office needs to be prepared to facilitate a number of decision-making approaches—tailored to the specific situation.

*The Ballard family began their journey to more effective collective deci-*

sion-making by creating an inventory of all the predictable decisions they will likely make going forward. The family office helped by reviewing the trust deeds, operating agreements, and various policies. There are known junctures ahead that they will have to navigate. The next step is to group this list of decisions by complexity and parties involved. We are helping the family learn a number of decision-making approaches and determine which is most appropriate for each situation. Questions about this include:

- How much of a factor is time?

- How many people are involved?

- Are significant conflicts of interest present?

- How well informed are the decision-makers, or is there a disparity of understanding that needs to be balanced?

- Do those involved have actual authority to make the decision, or are they forming a view to guide the actual decision-maker (as often when the family members are beneficiaries of trusts)?

- Is the family prepared to take emotional ownership of the family office and engage in decision-making? This is a cultural shift from simply being a client.

They have agreed to always include a facilitator when working on their most complex decisions. This ensures they are aware of the biases that might be at work

---

[44] Fist to Five voting introduces a scale of support in voting beyond a simple yes or no. By holding up a number of fingers from 5, for total enthusiasm, down to a fist, for vehement opposition, family members can show the degree of their support for a proposition.

*and will need to be actively countered in their thinking. It also ensures they do not rush the process, meaning they don't start with just two options and never rush to consensus. Instead, they spend time ideating on alternative solutions to be considered and consistently take time to allow different perspectives to be heard and understood.*

*They are now practicing. They have adopted some new tools, including the "fist to five" voting system[44] to provide insight into everyone's degree of support for the outcome. They have begun to take up decisions in their meetings with new intention and recognize the need to get good at decision-making together.*

## Intellectual Capital

A family's intellectual capital is its ability to function as a perpetual learning system which MIT professor Peter Senge defines as one that can both acquire new knowledge AND modify its behavior to reflect this new learning.[45]

This two-part definition clarifies several aspects of learning in families. First, it is never over. Learning needs to be integrated into the very fabric of the family, and its family office, from the team, working there through all the family members, not just the rising generation. Second, the learning journey isn't over once knowledge is acquired. Learning only has an impact when it is put into action.

Finally, the learning that forms the building block of a family's intellectual capital is much broader than traditional academics. While

---

[45] Senge, P. M. (2006). The Fifth Discipline: The art and practice of the learning organization. Broadway Business.

[46] See ViaCharacter.org for an assessment of 24 Character Strengths.

there is plenty of technical "know-how" that family members need to understand their economic capital, much broader competencies are involved in being good stewards of the family's true wealth. The more qualitative attributes include reflective listening, thinking, relating, collaborating, and managing ego and fears.

Every family member has different strengths,[46] and it is important to identify and nurture these as part of building a learning system. The family should adopt multiple learning modalities (visual, auditory, and kinesthetic) and a variety of approaches (active, cohort, inclusive) that invite family learners to tap into all their faculties and experience peer learning. Some of the best learning occurs when teaching new learnings to another or when a learner reflects on the takeaways from a recent experience or difficulty.

Another critical component of a family learning system is an intentional shift away from a traditional performance mindset where perfection and mastery are the measures of success. A performance focus is the antithesis of a learning mindset that embraces exploration, experimentation, and invention, where surprise outcomes are seen as fuel for learning rather than mistakes. A performance focus shifts attention to qualitative attributes (asking great questions) rather than quantitative (getting perfect scores).

Creating a learning system for the family allows the members to focus on the things humans do better than machines – including high-er-order critical thinking, innovation, creativity, relationship building,

---

[47] Humility is the New Smart, Edward D. Hess and Katherine Ludwig.

and collaboration.[47] These are the activities that empower a family to not just adapt to a changing world but to capitalize on the new opportunities it presents.

The most important trend in helping family offices transform their platforms into a learning system is the addition of a Chief Learning Officer. CLOs help family members think deeply about their assumptions and beliefs, values, and implicit rules they may be operating under. CLOs vary from a full-time position to bringing in outside consultants to fill the CLO role.

CLOs are equipped with a qualitative skill set very different from their more technically focused subject-matter experts in the family office. And they are constantly adding to their toolboxes (as good life-long learners do)! Some of the skills a CLO is working on and bringing to the family are communication, consensus building, planning, broadening perspective, managing conflict, collaborative decision-making, etc.

The Ballard family recognized early on that their previous approach to learning in the family was far too limited. They had focused only on their rising gen members as they came of age, and they had largely focused on training only around the family's financial capital. They realized they needed to establish a real budget for this work, and they would need to staff it and prioritize its oversight.

Initially, they used the family meetings as their learning laboratory, where they were introduced to great thought leaders in the field of family development. And over time, they have expanded their family office platform to take a much more substantive role in this work. They hired a Chief Learning Officer who is focused on growing the family members as well as the family office team. The CLO is working with each family member on their personal development, as well as crafting cohort learning opportunities where trust and collaboration can grow. The family has reviewed their team of consultants and advisors with an eye toward working with those who are committed to their personal development and supporting the priority of qualitative development in the family.

They have created an incubator for business ideas and invited thinkers and inventors from a vast and diverse group in the community to participate. They go on due diligence trips to remote parts of their home country, as well as internationally, in an effort to ensure they are more aware of the realities of other parts of the world.

The family is careful to balance the demands of each family member's time and to match their expectations to each individual's dreams and developmental goals. They seek ways to support and encourage without enabling or over-functioning. That means embracing desirable difficulties and celebrating the struggle. This is much harder to do than to say! Creating a culture where failure is seen as feedback, not a negative, is important and hard. This family starts every family meeting by going around the room to ask, "what have you failed at since we last met?" They have created the expectation that they are not pushing themselves to grow if each has not failed at something. Talk about a learning mindset!

These four intangible capitals and their related questions provide a measuring framework for a family office seeking to grow these qualitative capacities in the family it serves.

Table: The Four Intangible Capitals.

| Human Capital | Spiritual Capital | Social Capital | Intellectual Capital |
|---|---|---|---|
| Is every member striving to achieve his or her highest purpose and to bring their own dream to life? | Does the family have a transcendent purpose? | Does the family make timely decisions under pressure, be it internal or external? | Is the family a perpetual learning system — drawing on the unique gifts of each member? |
| Measured by the flourishing of every family member and the collective well-being of the family. | Often grounded in an intention that, together, they will seek to enhance the journeys of each member toward the whole family thriving. | This starts with the family's ability to make decisions and broadens to the family's ability to extend their reach to be in service of something bigger than themselves. | The family's ability to acquire new knowledge, share it among its members and then, most importantly, integrate it into its behaviors and competencies is the true measure of a learning system! |

Bringing these four qualitative capitals to life for a family involves a significant shift in mindset that starts with the family establishing the growth of its intangible capital as a priority and then executing these through the budgeting, staffing, and culture of their family office. This is no small undertaking. To date, a small cohort of early-adopter families is fully implementing this approach in their family offices.

## Practice. Practice. Practice.

While society widely embraces the importance of physical fitness in our daily lives to ensure our health and wellness, relatively few members of the population practice a daily fitness regimen. Similarly, it is easy to embrace developmental learning in our families intellectually. The reality is that only some are doing this. And while it has yet to be widely adopted, there is no question about the impact of helping each family member evolve developmentally and helping the family system function more effectively.

## With a qualitative focus, a family asks their family office to:

- Understand and help manage the family's group dynamics.

- Encourage all members to invest time and effort in understanding each other.

- Working to overcome tensions that can drive members to shut down or withdraw.

- Helping facilitate the rebuilding of damaged relationships between members.

- Equip the family with a dynamic process for decision-making and a system for practicing these skills.

- Build a system of communications that provides appropriate transparency, accountability, and feedback.

- Advocate for process, but remain "content neutral."

- Build and enable a family learning system.

- Provide tools for assessing where the family is today on its individual and collective developmental journey, helping them agree on goals and assist in monitoring progress.

- Help ensure family members participate in designing and owning their individual and family solutions.

- Inviting differences—in perspectives, opinions, and goals.

- Catalyze experimentation and celebrating unexpected outcomes.

- Help the family diversify its thinking, its community, and its team.

- Harness the intellectual capital & goodwill of all members.

- Recognize that family members start in different places and progress at different rates. Embrace and nurture these differences and meet each family member where they are.

## Yes, the Money Needs to Be Managed, Too

A family office still is responsible for managing the financial capital of the family, which involves great complexity and requires tremendous expertise.

Integrating a focus on the four qualitative capitals with the quantitative capital (the money) is critical. And interestingly, creating competencies around the intangible family assets helps with some of the particular challenges that come with money.

For example, financial wealth can be insulating and isolating. A family office can help create spaces where the family can be open and aware of the world outside their cocoon. An example would be creating learning forums where a broad community is invited to explore a common challenge. When hiring or engaging advisors, consider the opportunities they can provide as a source of diversity.

The financial wealth generated by an ancestor can create a sense of inadequacy in descendants. With that often comes an aversion to taking any risks or changing anything for fear of "screwing up" what has been the source of the family's economic capital. Families can leverage their family office for exploration and humble inquiry. It can be a place to take the right-sized risks to facilitate learning and help all reframe the meaning of F.A.I.L. to be "First Attempt Is Learning."

Embracing this holistic approach to the family's capital ensures that its wealth is truly framed in the context of the well-being of the family members. A family that shares a transcendent sense of purpose, where all members are flourishing, with the ability to collaborate and make decisions together, and is committed to integrating its on-going learning will be uniquely equipped to face a rapidly changing economy and contribute to new solutions and the exciting opportunities it presents.

## Reflection Questions

### Does your family have the patience to undertake this process?

This is a process, not an event. It is a continuing focus over the years and generations. Not everyone in the family is ready at the same time, and not everyone progresses at the same rate. And qualitative growth does not lend itself to easy numeric measures. That is not a reason to ignore it!

### Has your family office and advisor team done the work?

Learning and development start with each individual in the system, so it is not limited to the family members. Look at your family office employees and your advisors and consider: Have they embraced a beginner's mind, and are they working on their development?

### How do you establish the level of family engagement?

Taking a "Field of Dreams" approach—that "*If we build it, they will come*"—may not work. Implementing a culture of learning will require creativity and flexibility to adapt to individual readiness and capacity. Among the tools used are micro learnings, gamification, and multiple modalities of learning, including experiential and cohort learning. Focus on less input, more output (a core principle of learning science, meaning we need to make things less passive and more active.)[48]

## Does your family have the courage to balance the polarity of support and challenge?

Balancing this polarity is key to promoting growth for each family member. Yet, FO leaders we've collaborated with have self-identified that they have a natural tendency to enable family members without ensuring the balance of the right-sized challenge—also known as desirable difficulty.[49] This makes sense as it is natural to favor one pole out of concern for the downside of the opposite pole. Have you made clear to your family office that the family seeks to build competencies through experience, struggle, and failure? This requires communicating clear expectations that the FO does not enable or over-compensate for family members.

### Key Messages

- Learning is critical to adapting to this rapidly changing world.

- Family Offices have the potential to provide a world-class learning platform.

- But this requires a significant change in FO culture to embrace growing human capital as an existential priority.

- This dramatic change requires family member leadership and commitment to be effective.

---

[48] Make it Stick: The Science of Successful Learning, Peter C. Brown, Henry L. Roediger III, Mark A. McDaniel, 2014.

[49] Term coined in 1994 by UCLA Psychology Professor Robert (Bob) Bjork. A. McDaniel, 2014.

# 6

# The Antidote to Private Equity

## By Paul Carbone

**Johnson Generator Inc. had been at the center** of the Johnson family's personal and professional worlds for three generations. When the family sold their business, they were advised to form a family office and to allocate their now liquid capital to a group of third-party managers. Most Johnson family members wanted to be active in the family office, and they hired a small professional staff to help them with their family services and family investing. After that, the family office became the new organizational center for the Johnson family. Unfortunately, during the ten years following the sale of their operating business, the family ties frayed, and family members increasingly moved in their own directions. In particular, the next generation of the family was becoming increasingly disenchanted with their limited influence and the limited impact of their capital. In addition, the family's passive investment portfolio struggled to perform and did not achieve the sustained returns the family generated from their former operating business. The Johnson family had transformed its family capital in the form of an operating business which had given the family mission, purpose, and attractive returns into passive, mission-less financial capital, which now was represented merely by numbers on a financial statement. The inherent advantages of Johnson's family capital had been lost in its transformation to just a financial asset structured like all other institutional financial assets.

The Johnson family story is fictional, but this is the real-life story of countless families who have transitioned from their long-standing family enterprise to become passive family investors in traditional family office structures. The Johnson family is the composite of many families who have struggled during the period after their family business. Some family business owners rightfully recognize the peril for their family during the period after their family business and become frozen in their decision-making when it's clear that the family business must be sold for competitive, asset diversification, or other reasons.

"Families often struggle with the transition away from their family business, and those struggles only multiply once the family is on the other side of that transition," says Francois M. de Visscher of de Visscher Advisors LLC and co-founder of FODIS, a long-standing advisor to families and family businesses as well as a member of a multi-generational family which owns a sizeable European business. He adds that "the complexities of family transitions are further complicated by the younger generation of family members who often have very different expetations of wealth and its ability to facilitate change."

No doubt, owning a family business is no panacea for all families. By intermingling complicated family dynamics with the commercial realities of business today, family business ownership inevitably creates challenges and strife. However, when families like the Johnsons decide to sell their family business and form a family office, they are wise to recognize that the operating asset they once owned was valuable to the family beyond the business' purely financial benefit.

Families, through their family offices, are advantaged in multiple ways by being active direct deployers of their family capital and active investors in operating businesses. By doing so and avoiding becoming purely financial, passive investors, families can address some of the fundamental design flaws of traditional family offices. (See Design Flaws.)

In particular, families lose a sense of purpose and emotional ownership when they become primarily passive capital deployers. (See Andrew Keyt's chapter about The Transformative Family Office.) By deploying their capital in passive form in traditional structures, families also give up the inherent advantages of their family capital and forgo attractive opportunities. Finally, traditional family office structures with passive approaches often lack agility and creativity in responding to the market's changing needs.

As a result, families don't pursue the alternate systems and processes necessary to adapt to rapidly changing market demands and fail to maximize their opportunities as investors and as families.

The Johnson family story is indicative of an inherent challenge even in the most basic of family office functions. There are many purposes to a family office. Wealth management is necessary for many family offices among the other technical needs and higher objectives. However, even within the very pedestrian family office function of wealth management, how families engage with their capital as well as manage and deploy it can have fundamental implications for the family. The family approach to wealth management can either enhance or erode the family dynamic as well as either support or undermine the family's other positive family office initiatives.

There are various approaches to family office wealth management. But capturing the essence of direct investment, active family involvement and ownership can be the strategic necessity to maintaining appropriate alignment between a family and its purpose, values, and goals as well as to generating above-market returns.

## Recapture Family Legacy

Today, capital is abundant and commoditized, resulting in the investment market being massively competitive and generally undifferentiated. The market is awash with third-party traditional capital managers who are primarily asset gathers of "other people's money" or OPM. These third-party managers often use traditional capital deployment business models in a fund structure. Traditional fund structures are typically short-term, tightly defined, and generally focused only on financial return.

Using a traditional, passive capital approach to having their financial capital managed by outside managers, family capital owners can quickly become distant from the impact of their capital and lose the ability to have a direct and tangible way of creating social benefit. The third-party, passive, and more rigid approach to capital deployment could not be more distinct from how many families made their wealth to begin with—by starting, building, and enhancing family businesses. Families, through their family businesses, have an active involvement with their employees and their families; their customers, suppliers, and even competitors; and, significantly, with their communities, industries, and business associations. A family's engagement with other family members and with the world around them fundamentally changes when they merely review their wealth on family office spreadsheets. (See the chart in Jill Shipley's chapter comparing the typical mindset of a family business with that of a family office.)

The solution to these unique family challenges and opportunities is clear— families should recapture their legacy. Not only can they recapture their legacy by again becoming owners of/investors in operating businesses, but families should use this newfound approach of actively investing their capital in charting a new, exciting future for their families.

The Larry H. Miller family of Utah did precisely that. In 2009, Larry H. Miller passed away, leaving to his wife, Gail Miller, their entire estate of car dealerships, the Salt Lake Bees, a movie theater chain, and the Utah Jazz, among other assets.

As of 2022, the Miller family sold some of these assets, creating meaningful liquidity. Rather than only passively investing this newfound liquidity, the family deliberately began to acquire a new group of operating companies oriented to the family's values, current interests, and excitement for today's growth industries.

Steve Starks, CEO of the Larry H. Miller Company, said that "rebuilding a group of operating assets was an explicit decision by the Millers as they believed that the family would be stronger if they were organized around and involved with operating companies. They viewed having a group of operating businesses as a unifying mechanism."

If families have the right strategy, team, and tactics, as well as sufficient capital and a longer duration timeline, they should maintain or develop an active, direct deployment business model. Families need to put their capital back into operating businesses that align with their values and be at the core of this effort. They must be actively engaged in this process to fully rekindle their family passions and philosophies.

Direct deployment and business ownership (as majority or minority investors) do not need to be the family's exclusive investment approach, but it should be an essential element of their overall family office and investment philosophy. Sometimes multi-generational trusts or cultural limitations create impediments to a direct deployment strategy. However, even operating within structural or self-imposed constraints, families should seek to develop and emphasize any element of a direct deployment approach which would help move the family along in the spectrum from passive to active investor.

## Family Capital: Sources and Uses

What does the family market need to recognize before this solution can be implemented? Families with capital to invest need to acknowledge the dramatic changes underway in the investing market and among family offices, particularly the challenges to the traditional family office model. They need to recognize the insidious erosion of their family values and engagement, which can come from the passive investing model. In addition, families with capital to invest need to realize that the next generation of family members likely will have different expectations and requirements for their capital, further challenging traditional family office models and pushing families to invest with purpose and impact. Finally, families need to advocate for the inherent advantages of their capital and assume a more public profile in executing a more active family direct investment model.

At the same time, families looking for capital for their family businesses need to recognize that all capital is not the same and the likely superiority of family capital as a source of capital for their businesses and, thereby, their own families. These families need to understand that their advisors and family office professionals need to be educated and similarly recognize the full scope of the changes, opportunities, and challenges both in the traditional family office model and with an active, direct investment program.

## The Caution

This direct, active approach to family investing does not come without cost or risk. The direct deployment family office model will require an entirely different mindset as well as different processes, teams, and resources versus a passive investment model. The direct deployment family office team needs other skills, expertise, and knowledge. As discussed in the chapter by Jill Barber and Greg McCann, the family likely will need to find teams with greater capacity and agility than they typically have today. Finding and retaining this talent can take time and effort. Developing and implementing these capabilities also will necessitate a shift in the family's risk tolerance and likely public profile.

Family business ownership can be a source of tension and is not just a straightforward solution to family cohesion. Family business history is replete with examples of families that have fractured because of disagreements regarding how a family business should be run. Sometimes, families need to liberate themselves from the demands of family business ownership to find a constructive and productive way forward for the family.

If a family does choose the direct deployment model, they should have clear, agreed guidelines on governance, liquidity plans, timelines, and defined family member opt-in/opt-out mechanics before embarking on this often rewarding but sometimes treacherous path. As Andrew Keyt recommends in his chapter, in all cases, the family must build its efforts on the solid foundation of a well-thought-out strategic plan.

## The Way Forward

If done correctly, family direct investing can help families more effectively achieve their goals, enhance the investing market, build better businesses and even address societal challenges.

Within the private equity market, families can help create, define, and build an entirely new and distinct sub-asset class of family direct investing. By employing a direct investment strategy, families can reclaim their sense of purpose and regain a cohesiveness not achievable through a passive strategy. They can build better, more competitive, and sustainable companies which generate higher, long-term returns on their capital. They can engage and motivate the next generation of family members in ways not possible with a passive approach.

Importantly, when there is purpose and action, through their companies, families also can effectively begin to address some of humankind's most perplexing and difficult challenges. To accomplish these laudable goals, families should be much more aggressive in collaborating, educating, advocating, and organizing to advance the new family investing model, including forming trade associations, funding lobbying efforts, and implementing media campaigns.

In our example above, all is not lost for the Johnson family, as the way forward is clear for them as a family and investors. The adverse effects of passively investing capital can likely be reversed. The Johnson family does not need to try to recreate Johnson Generator, but it does need to reinvent the benefits derived from their active involvement with their former business. This can be done with effort, focus and discipline, and many families today are doing just that.

## Realigning the Misaligned

Families risk having their financial capital misaligned with their overall purpose, values, and goals when they pursue narrow, short-term, passive approaches to deploying their capital. This misalignment will likely steadily erode family cohesion as family purpose dissipates.

## The Capital Picture

The world is awash in capital. Today, capital is abundant and commoditized, creating massively competitive investing markets. SIFMA estimates that in 2021 the global debt and equity capital markets totaled approximately $250 trillion, with the institutional or traditional market representing a significant percentage of the global market.

Much of the capital from traditional sources comes with constraints and limitations imposed on the ultimate capital owner/investor. Investors interested in the institutional market are asked to invest in standard and highly regulated fund structures. Traditional capital providers must deploy consistent with these time-limited business models, often using well-defined criteria and approaches that encourage short-term financial return and capital velocity.

The objectives for this capital often are narrowly gauged with anything but lofty financial or social expectations. Often traditional sources of capital see the businesses they invest as poker chips on the gambling table or as blinking lights on a computer screen. The institutional goal is to create a quick return rather than necessarily to build great, long-lasting companies which address fundamental needs and deliver social benefit. This mindset is often antithetical to how many families run their businesses and build wealth.

A sub-market within the broader capital market is the direct invest private capital market. The three primary sources of direct investment private capital for businesses are traditional private capital funds, strategic acquirers (often publicly traded companies), and families/family offices.

Preqin estimates that global assets under management in private capital funds, encompassing private equity and private credit funds, will double by 2027. Specifically, Preqin forecasts assets will rise to $18.3 trillion by 2027 from $9.3 trillion in 2021. In looking at just the traditional private equity market, Preqin forecasts this market to exceed $6 trillion in 2022. PitchBook estimates that US private equity firms own more than 10,000 businesses in their portfolios today.

In terms of the family office market, Campden Research estimates that over 7,000 family offices worldwide in 2019 managed nearly $6 trillion. Accounting firm EY estimates that today there are more than 10,000 family offices globally that manage the wealth of a single family, implying a significant increase in the total capital managed by families.

## The Superiority of Family Capital and Direct Investing

When families allocate their capital to third-party managers like private equity funds or invest in publicly traded companies, they immediately become passive participants giving away their discretion and active involvement. Their capital becomes numbers on a piece of paper or a computer screen. Capital becomes lifeless and soulless. When families cede active involvement with their capital, they often undermine the family's sense of purpose and cohesiveness.

Steve Starks from the Larry H. Miller Company reinforced this perspective.

"After the Miller family had sold the most well-known of their operating businesses and generated significant liquidity," he said, "the family decided that allocating much of this capital to third-party managers was not as helpful in building family unity as opposed to directly investing the family's capital again into operating businesses."

In being capital allocators, not family business owners, purpose solely becomes about returns which only brings a limited sense of satisfaction. For next-generation family members, returns are often secondary to the pursuit of other higher goals.

Contrary to traditionally structured fund capital, family capital has maximum flexibility—given that it is both permanent (does not have to be returned by a specific date) and proprietary (it is the family's capital, and not Other People's Money or "OPM"). In many ways, family capital is unbounded and unconstrained, with an often complex, multi-faceted approach to achieving its goals and objectives. This capital also often comes imbued with a family ethos, philosophy, and value system absent in traditional sources of direct invest capital (traditional private equity funds or publicly traded companies). Family capital can be employed in active form to impact tangible, observable results directly. Family capital can be deployed to create attractive returns, generate social good, and align with (and not contradict) the family's philanthropic efforts. Both returns and the achievement of higher goals can be accomplished with family capital without sacrificing any aspect of either.

Family capital is effectively the antidote to the challenges of traditional private equity. If applied with the right strategy, team, and tactics, as well as in sufficient quantities and with the appropriate timeline, family capital can effectively address the fundamental and systemic deficiencies of traditionally structured capital. Because of its various advantages, family capital can present a differentiated and often more attractive option to users of capital versus most traditionally structured capital. By doing so, capital users who value those differences can materially benefit, and family capital providers can create a real competitive advantage versus most of the capital available from traditional sources. Higher-than-market returns often are realized when a deployer of capital can achieve an acknowledged competitive advantage in a commoditized market.

Families as direct deployers of family capital in operating businesses (often other family enterprises) can generate higher returns and sustain higher returns. Because of the inherent advantages of their capital to business owners, family capital providers can systematically and consistently find better investment opportunities and prevail with a higher frequency in winning those opportunities.

Despite its limitations, constraints, and disadvantages, there is no doubt that traditional private equity has long been a massively successful business model. Over the last ten years, according to J.P. Morgan Asset Management, traditional private equity has generated higher returns versus most other asset classes other than possibly venture capital.

However, given their inherent advantages, direct deployers of family capital have the opportunity to generate superior returns even to the lofty results generated by traditional private equity. Laura Van Peenan, Global Head of Alternative Private Equity at William Blair, highlights that many business owners prefer to achieve their liquidity and growth goals by partnering with family investors rather than private equity firms or other capital providers. She observes, "the appeal of family investors can be based on several factors, including their appreciation for the legacy and values of the business and its original owners; their long-term perspective and ownership timeframes; their interest in truly partnering with the management team, employees and family members who will continue with the business; their regard for the broader community and philanthropic interests that are important to the company; and their conservatism regarding debt."

Versus traditional private equity, family capital providers also can build better, more competitive, and sustainable companies. Families are not bound by the time-limited traditional private equity business model constraints. They can focus on the critical and ignore the expedient. They can make the right decisions for the right reasons and in the right timeframe. Their objectives can be exclusively focused on creating a better business. For families, the journey can be as important as the destination. Compared to traditional private equity, family investors do not have to be mindful of creating liquidity for investors in the short term to facilitate fundraising for the next fund.

"Families have the luxury of time in building businesses to their standards and objectives and not to the expectations of third-party financial investors who may have different investment objectives," says Ryan Harris, Co-Head of Kirkland & Ellis' Private Investment & Family Office group. "As a result, in building their business and being able to prioritize both mission-driven and family objectives, as well as a longer-term investment strategy, families often have the opportunity to end up at a higher point on the mountain with a strong, generationally sustainable business."

Families can reclaim their sense of purpose and family cohesion by being direct deployers in businesses and minimizing passive investing. They can consistently generate attractive returns and can make concrete their direct impact on employees, employee families, customers/suppliers, and their broader communities. They can ensure that their companies operate in sustainable ways to have a sustainable impact on some of humankind's most complex challenges (the environment, economic inequality, etc.). Importantly, in the direct deployment model, families can better engage and actively involve the next generation and address their growing interest in using their capital with a strong intent of having an impact.

## Family Capital and the Evolution of Direct Investing

Families have been using the benefits of family capital to build their businesses for centuries. Similarly, families have long provided family capital to other family businesses for mutual benefit.

Families seeking the benefit of investing in private companies have vastly different capabilities, resources, expertise, and expectations. As a result, families have taken varied approaches to their investing and ended up at various points along the spectrum, from indirect, passive investing to direct, active investing.

Moreover, these approaches and where families fall on the investing spectrum have evolved as family investors have become more sophisticated and the private capital market has matured.

Early in their journey to gain access to private companies, some families took the less direct approach of investing in traditional private equity funds, which is a less effective approach but one that gave families exposure to the private market. This fund-investing approach was often complemented by making discretionary co-investments alongside the fund directly in companies managed by the fund.

Some families who wanted even more direct exposure decided to either invest as a minority owner behind another lead family investor or pool their capital and capabilities with multiple similarly interested families to form family syndicates to invest directly in companies. Other families chose to invest behind "independent or fundless sponsors" who brought them investment opportunities and proposed to oversee the companies post-close.

Finally, on the other end of the investing approach spectrum, some families decided to assemble their own professional investing teams and to be a lead investor—source, evaluate, and oversee—in private companies.

During the last decade, the migration of families along the investing spectrum from indirect private equity fund investors to family direct investor has accelerated. "[Among family offices], funds are still popular but investing in individual companies…is even more popular," says the founder of private equity advisor Triago, Antoine Drean.

According to the UBS 2022 Global Family Office Report, in the next five years, 42% of family offices surveyed expect to boost their allocation to direct investing. This direct invest interest among families is accelerating. In 2019, families surveyed by UBS allocated 9 percent of their capital to direct private equity versus 7 percent to private equity funds and fund-of-funds. In 2021, direct investing increased to 13 percent of assets while investments in funds stayed relatively flat at 8 percent.

Max Kunkel, chief investment officer for UBS' Global Family and Institutional Wealth division, said that family offices leaned more to direct investing as they see it "as an extension of the entrepreneurial activities of the principal" and no doubt as a return to their roots as a family.

Similarly, Citi Private Bank's 2022 Family Office Survey indicated that 29 percent of family offices allocated between 10 percent and 20 percent of their portfolios to direct investing, while another 35 percent allocated more than 30 percent. Citi's survey goes on to indicate that family offices have become more flexible in terms of their preferences for types of direct investing, with controlling stakes (defined as ownership of 25 percent or more) representing 37 percent of surveyed family offices, followed by passive investments (24 percent) and minority investing (19 percent). Further, family offices strongly preferred direct or co-investments (72 percent) over other alternatives like partnership investing.

However, today's capital markets present different challenges and opportunities for family investors. As mentioned above, the massive liquidity and over-capitalization of the market and the related hyper-competitiveness of investing are at an extreme today.

As a result, and out of necessity, an increasing number of families are executing an alternative, more sophisticated approach to family investing deemed necessary to achieve family investing goals. These approaches are very different from the traditional family investing model and often involve adopting the best practices and approaches of sophisticated traditional investors while maintaining the best of family investing. High-profile families taking this alternative approach to deploy their capital include the Pritzker family, the Michael Dell family, and the Paul Allen estate, among others.

The alternative models these families employ are varied as each family attempts to match its specific goals and objectives to a structure that allows the family to compete and win in today's competitive marketplace. Some of these families use scale, breadth, and sophistication to address the market including the Walton, Gates, and Johnson families. Some use alternate structures which employ third-party capital alongside family capital to enhance their reach into the market as well as improve their ability to attract and retain a talented team. These families would include the Pritzkers and Dell families. Some families partner across generations or with other like-minded families or with public market investors to create both public and private investment groups with sufficient capital and scale to compete. These groups include Eurazeo, Wendel, and Cobepa.

These same families also are advocating the inherent advantages of their capital and are assuming a more public profile in the execution of a more active family direct invest model. They are educating intermediaries, lenders, and advisors and bringing into the family industry skilled family office professionals who understand the needs, challenges, and opportunities of the new family office model. By doing so, they are advancing the cause of family direct investing among all market participants.

## Family Direct Investing: Challenges and Risks

Despite all of the potential benefits, there are real cautions for deployers of family capital and those families interested in being active direct deployers in businesses. Having maximum flexibility as a family capital investor has many advantages but that flexibility also can be a hindrance. Having the flexibility of family capital does not mean that families should use all degrees of the flexibility at their disposal. In particular, investing in all manner of securities, industries, and markets, especially without the commensurate expertise, can mean both dispersion of effort and a reversion to mean returns or worse.

As mentioned previously, family capital can quickly lose its advantage if simply invested into passive structured vehicles with too many constraints (even if the capital is then invested in companies). The structure itself diffuses most of the benefits of family capital.

In addition, a family's intent, relative to direct investing, is certainly necessary but not generally sufficient to guarantee success. Francois de Visscher notes that "over the generations, a number of families with substantial wealth sometimes alternate their approach to wealth management between passive investing and active investing, between being purely financial investors and being direct investors in operating businesses. Mr. de Visscher explained that one reason for this phenomenon is that "direct investing requires a family commitment and expertise which is not always present in every generation."

Importantly, once a family decides that they want to be active direct deployers of capital and investors directly in businesses, their journey has only just begun. Success is only ensured by applying an appropriate investing strategy with a well-understood set of consistent objectives implemented by a qualified, aligned team using the right process and procedures.

Family direct investing is generally a more difficult approach versus passive investing requiring meaningfully different skills, expertise, risk tolerance, and capability. Sufficient scale, staying power, and a willingness to take a more public profile also are minimum conditions for a family to build a dedicated, captive family direct invest business.

The professional team working alongside the family is key to the success of a direct family invest strategy. Hiring the right team with the requisite skills is critical. The professional team's cultural compatibility and philosophical consistency with the family have to be a given. Again, even with the right team, the family cannot be passive participants but must be engaged partners. Finally, the family needs to develop and implement the right alignment and incentive programs to ensure that the professional team's behavior and decision making is in lockstep with the family's goals and objectives. The family can have the best of intentions, but if their professional team behaves and invests like traditional capital providers, they will massively diminish their family capital advantages.

To put a finer point on the challenges of team alignment and incentive, here are two examples where families failed to carefully match strategy, objectives, and an appropriately incentivized team all to disastrous results.

First, Family A is a European family which publicly prided itself on having a "one-hundred-year investing cycle". They were convinced that they should and could invest across multiple generations for the long-term benefit of the family. However, the professional team they hired only realized bonus above base salaries upon the sale of their company investments. Teams will execute to their incentive and, needless to say, this team ended up investing for a much shorter duration than one hundred years.

A second example relates to Family B, a US family, which allocated an amount of capital to a direct invest program, assembled a team, and proceeded to begin investing. After a few years, the team did as they were directed and deployed most of their initial capital allocation in a portfolio of companies. However, the family decided that they wanted to slow the pace of investing and did not allocate additional capital to the program. Shortly after making that decision, the family lost most of its professional team to other firms still actively investing and ended up having a portfolio of companies to oversee without a team to do it.

Family business ownership alone is no panacea for the ills of family disengagement or passive investing. Family direct investing requires discipline and years of hard work to bear fruit. Before pursuing a family direct invest program, families should have clear, agreed guidelines on governance, succession, liquidity, and timelines with defined family member opt-in or opt-out mechanics.

## A Measured Approach

Moreover, structural, cultural and expertise limitations may demand that a direct investing program applies to only some of a family's capital or that the family take a gradual, phased-in approach to implement their desired direct invest program.

The Laird Norton Company represents a terrific example of a family group that took a disciplined, patient, but concerted path toward implementing a direct invest effort. The Laird Norton Company is a seventh-generation family-owned enterprise that "provides long-term capital and resources to empower companies to thrive." Family member, Laird Koldyke, describes the family's approach as a journey where the family first sought outside expertise, an experienced partner, to help teach the family the tactics and approaches to successful direct investing.

Laird Norton Company has long operated a number of significant businesses. After the family sold one of their major operating assets generating significant liquidity for the family and company, the family and company senior management made the decision to develop an internal direct invest capability to buy new businesses. Not having an internal investing team or skills, the company decided to partner with a traditional PE firm with the explicit agenda of learning to invest.

From this partnership, the family and senior management learned what was required to find, review, and win opportunities in a competitive market. The family also learned the critical importance of having the right team using the right practices with the right objectives. "The family learned to walk before it ran with its direct invest program. We wanted to be fully educated on what was required to be a successful investor before committing meaningful capital," said Mr. Koldyke. One particular benefit that Mr. Koldyke highlighted was that the family learned that the initial sticker shock associated with the cost of hiring a talented investing team quickly dissipated when the family fully understood their critical importance in a successful investing effort.

## The Future is Bright

Family direct investing can help families more effectively achieve their goals, align their capital with their mission, enhance the investing market, build better businesses, and begin to address societal challenges. Within the private equity market, families can help create, define, and build an entirely distinct and often superior sub-asset class of family direct investing.

By employing a direct invest strategy, families also can reclaim their sense of purpose and regain a cohesiveness not achievable through a passive strategy. They can build better, more competitive, and sustainable companies as well as generate higher, long-term returns on their capital. They can engage and motivate the next generation of family members in ways not possible with a passive approach. Finally, and importantly, families can more effectively begin to address some of humankind's most perplexing and difficult challenges.

To accomplish these laudable goals, families should be much more aggressive in collaborating, educating, advocating, and organizing to advance the new family investing model including forming trade associations, funding lobbying efforts, and implementing media campaigns.

Family capital has inherent advantages over the passive model and, in particular, over traditional private equity capital. However, the traditional private equity model is a massively successful model in its own right having generated attractive returns over many years for its many investors both individual and institutional. Traditional private equity is also a mature market with participants actively looking to innovate and find their own competitive advantage. Increasingly, the traditional private equity firm is recognizing the advantages of flexible, long-dated family capital and adopting structures and approaches in an attempt to duplicate those advantages.

The traditional private equity market has seen growth in permanent investing vehicles, hybrid family/traditional PE models, and the GP-led continuation vehicles. Will traditional PE significantly co-opt the family direct invest market minimizing its differentiation and advantage? Unlikely but capital providers are continuously looking for an advantage in a non-differentiated market. Family capital and the direct invest model is clearly a competitively advantaged model and no doubt will have many who try to mimic its benefits.

There is hope for our fictional Johnson family as the benefits of family capital become ever more clear throughout the direct investing ecosystem. Moreover, the path for families interested in again becoming direct investors and owners of businesses is being further defined and refined by more families each year. The progress being made by alternative family direct investors is accelerating and, if they seize the opportunity, the future is bright for families like the Johnson family.

## Reflection Questions

- How should family members best get involved in a direct investing program? What if they initially do not have the requisite skills, interest, or capability? What role is best suited for the family team—board level, investment committee, tactical deal doing and/or company operational oversight?

- How can this direct investing effort best support the entrepreneurial initiatives of the next generation family member?

- To best align interests and to help ensure retention, how should the family think about sharing with their investing team both the risk and rewards of an investment program? What about the sharing of decision-making authority?

- How does a next-generation "impact" oriented investing program fit within an overall profit-focused investing effort?

- How can similarly interested family groups work together to best accomplish their shared goals and objectives?

# CHAPTER 7

## Voices of the Field

**Even the most thoughtful, innovative,** and collaborative people, including those who have contributed chapters to this book, can sometimes miss the mark in their analysis. For that reason, we decided to host a gathering of families, family office executives, and advisors—a representation of the field we hope to reach—to discuss the ideas presented in this book and learn from their breadth of experience. We were delighted by the enthusiastic response we received and the insightful comments they offered.

We met on Friday, September 9, 2022, at Aileron in Dayton, Ohio.

Aileron is a nonprofit organization that believes professional management—a systematic way to run a business for long-term sustainability and growth—can empower organizations to thrive in any environment. They have been helping business owners, leaders, and teams harness the power of professional management for over 25 years. Their campus offers a beautiful respite from the day-to-day hustle and was a perfect setting for our conversation.

After a delicious breakfast and tour of the campus led by Joni Fedders, the President of Aileron and contributor to this book, co-editors Greg McCann and Jill Barber kicked off the event and thanked everyone for their willingness to lend their insights into the critical topic of unlocking the potential of the single family office.

Greg explained that the day's goal was to hear their candid feedback about the ideas presented in this book. He also explained that we would represent the voices of the field in this chapter without attribution so everyone could feel comfortable being as forthright as possible.

The basic structure of the day was as follows: Jill Shipley presented a big-picture overview of her chapter, "Wealth Perception Shapes Reality." After this, Jill Barber and Greg McCann presented the design flaws at the front of this book. These presentations led to a lively high-level discussion, followed by discussions of each chapter.

**This chapter provides 12 highlights of the day. We hope you find them as helpful as we did.**

## 1. The field's legacy is strong.

Countless families and family offices have made tremendous contributions to society over the decades. But unfortunately, many of these contributions are little known and celebrated because the families prefer to remain quiet about them. That, however, in no way diminishes the significance of the contributions made to date.

One participant said: "We have families that have done such amazing things in this country, which make the United States unique. Families have endowed hospitals, endowed research, endowed so much, and we've lost track of that."

There's a multitude of challenges within that perception. Many of the old-guard families don't want to be acknowledged. They don't want people to know they gave $100 million to this facility; they do it quietly. Some families don't tell their children and grandchildren what they've done.

"I asked one client to list their donations and share them at the family meeting. When they did that, there were tears because people in the family had no idea that the park they were walking in their family helped to build."

## 2. Now is an opportunity for single family offices to take the next step in their evolution.

This is an opportune time to lean into the next stage of evolution in the work of families and family offices. Many observers recognized a need and an appetite for fresh thinking about the untapped potential in the work of families and family offices. They also noted that most books about single family offices are essentially 101 guides about how to set them up and run them. This book, they said, brings the conversation to the next level.

As one participant said: "There is a readiness for change."

And another said: "This is about saying there's something more on the menu that you've not experienced yet, and that is this sphere of expertise you need. So, you're hiring the accountants; you're hiring the investment people. But there is another necessary ingredient for this to stay productive and make it that much better."

## 3. Different families have different levels of interest in using their resources to help make the world better.

It was recognized that not all families and family offices want to make the world a better place. Some will be satisfied with the status quo. Therefore, there should be no expectation that all families and family offices need to evolve.

As one participant said: "There are some families that are doing it well. Some are not doing it and are not interested. This book should interest people in the middle."

## 4. Many single family offices focus solely on the financial (or technical) over the non-financial (and human) because it is easier.

As one participant said: "I think we manage the money because it's easier to do it. And families do not want to step into the nonfinancial work because it appears there's no answer, there's no easy win."

Another said: "You can see how we end up with this problem because nobody likes to talk about the messy, thorny stuff. And so, it all just gets shoved under the rug."

5. **There are growing negative attitudes toward high-wealth-people.**

There was broad agreement that there appears to be a growth in negative attitudes toward high-income individuals and families. Some noted that politics and the media influence this. One participant said: "It's easy to unify around an enemy. And so the dialogue is about creating enemies rather than understanding."

6. **Many wealthy people do not think of themselves as rich. And it would be better if they did.**

It was observed that a significant number of people with wealth do not identify themselves as wealthy. It was also suggested that it is vital for single family offices and advisers to help them recognize that they are so that they can address the challenges brought about by the growing economic inequality in this country and the negative attitudes toward the wealthy that result.

As one participant said: "I think there should be an effort from us in the single family office to make them realize that yes, they are rich. And yes, there is inequality. They have to realize that to speak up; and if we make them aware of the situation and that it might not be sustainable, perhaps they will react more, and they will be able to speak up more."

7. **Technical roles currently carried out by family offices are essential. In no way should their importance be seen as diminished by this call to the next stage of evolution in the mission of families and family offices.**

As one participant said: "I keep coming back to the word "liminal," of saying, OK, we can build a technical base to keep it running. You have to meet us at some point. If you can't meet us at that point, this will stay a technical piece. And that's not bad. It's not bad if they do it with awareness."

## 8. Partnership is key.

The way to unlock the potential of this next stage of evolving the single family office was seen as resting on a partnership or interdependence between the family and the family office. Either one can take the lead. But ultimately, it requires the involvement of both the family and single family office because it is a symbiotic relationship.

There was also significant discussion about the function of the family office as centered around the family vision and the role of single family office leadership in cultivating and stewarding the humans in their care.

As one participant said, "When you get that right, the rest is execution."

## 9. Health of the family is also crucial.

There was significant discussion about the family's health being key to long-term sustainability—which requires cultivation and investment in relationships.

As one participant said: "One of the common paths to a family office is a liquidity event with a family business. And we've got the plan for stewarding the financial capital into the family office."

"But there's no model for that sense of purpose that the business gave, the impact on the people, the impact on the community that was such a unifying force for the family that brings family members together. And at the end of the day, sustainability will be directly correlated with the quality of the relationships within the family."

## 10. Single family office leaders should think freshly about the language they use.

Some participants spoke about the importance of getting away from defining the work of the single family office in terms of wealth alone.

One participant said: "We have been intentional about shifting the language we use. So, we're not in the wealth business. We're in the human business.

But the human pieces are just as important as the others. The wealth is in service to the rest. And so, I see the family offices as having a significant role in being able to champion this."

## 11. There are creative ways to engage younger generations.

There was a lively discussion about how to keep younger generations engaged. There was a fair amount of excitement around the idea of instituting a ritual of younger generations opting in or out of the family business every year. Part of the reason that some younger generations feel negatively, after all, is that they don't have a choice in being engaged. Presenting it as a choice could potentially change that.

## 12. Developing a learning culture is pivotal.

Developing a learning culture was pivotal to shifting from focusing on technical roles alone. Several observers encouraged investing in learning throughout the culture by creating a budget line or treating it like R&D. It would also help strengthen a commitment to learning since people tend to focus on what they can measure.

The biggest takeaway is that it can be done. There was significant enthusiasm for the case study of Jill Barber's work and how she created change as the leader of the single family office. Her example was described as *an oasis* because it demonstrated what can actually happen.

It was also recognized that there's a need to move from the sense that "the ideas presented in this book are great too, we could never do that" to yes, you can. Related to this, participants also agreed that the skills of capacity and agility advocated by Greg McCann are critical to this work.

## Additional Comments

"The authors' work was sound, and the feedback given by all just enhanced the work that had been put into each chapter. I loved how feedback and insight were not just welcomed; they were requested in a way that made everyone feel a sense of ownership in the book. Reflecting on the time together a month later, I have nothing but positive thoughts. I feel grateful to have spent the time with such a professional and engaging group of people."

—Tracy Kirkland Payne, Director and Treasurer, Family Office Services, Cockrell Interests, LLC

"It was simply amazing, and I learned so much and was able to really think in a different headspace, surrounded by all of the amazing talent and leaders in the room. I am very interested in keeping the group together."

—Christine Franco, President, Ingeborg

"It is a terrific group of like-minded folks who share a passion of helping others. I believe many of the conversations could have continued for a week! The body of work is impressive. It has inspired and re-energized my efforts to grow my advisory practice."

—Tim Volk, Founder and Principal, T. Volk & Co.

"It was humbling to be a part of an effort that will truly alter the course of how single family offices serve their clients. Family unity and cohesion are finding their place alongside more traditional financial measures of success for SFO clients, and I found the talent assembled to review this work was uniquely qualified to articulate how to achieve it."

—Tom White, Chairman & CEO, Haws Corporation

# Author Biographies

### Stacy Allred

A consultant in the Financial Services Industry. Stacy has spent the last three years as Managing Director and Head of Family Engagement and Governance at First Republic. Prior to joining First Republic in 2020, Ms. Allred spent twenty years with Merrill Private Wealth Management, founding the Merrill Center for Family Wealth™ during her time there. Previously, she provided comprehensive financial planning and tax services to multigenerational family groups and executives for nine years with Ernst & Young. Ms. Allred has dedicated her career to walking alongside individuals and families to more effectively navigate the complexity and promise of wealth. Immersed in the facilitation of family meetings, her practice includes the application of family governance and decision making, family dynamics, learning and development of the rising generation, philanthropy and transition planning.

### Jill Barber

President of CYMI Holdings (*cymiholdings.com*), which provides wealth advisory services to the Mathile family. As a member of CYMI since 1999, Jill has been involved in hundreds of successful business and philanthropic transactions that have helped the Mathile family to change the landscape of the Dayton region and several places around the world.

### Paul J. Carbone

Co-Founder and President of Pritzker Private Capital (*ppcpartners.com*). Pritzker Private Capital partners with entrepreneur- and family-owned middle-market companies with leading positions in the manufactured products and services sectors. Previously, Paul was the Director and Managing Partner of the Private Equity Group of Robert W. Baird & Co., which makes venture capital, growth equity and buyout investments in smaller, high-potential companies in the US, Europe, and Asia.

## James M. Coutré

Vice President of Insights & Connections for Fidelity Family Office Services, a segment of Fidelity Institutional (*fidelity. com*). Fidelity Family Office Services is the division of Fidelity Investments® which provides custody, brokerage, investment, and reporting services to family offices, ultra- wealthy families and the investment professionals that support them. Since its inception in 2004, the business has grown to be administrator of $140+ billion in assets on behalf of more than 400 ultra-high-net-worth families.

## Mary Duke

An internationally recognized advisor to families navigating the complexities of substantial wealth. She is known for her deep understanding of the impact of trusts and generational dynamics on families. Her work is anchored in the facilitation of family meetings, coaching & mediation for family members, and strategic planning for their owned enterprises. (*thehighrd.com*)

## Chris Ernst, Ph.D.

Chief Learning Officer at Workday (*workday.com*). As an executive, he has held senior leadership roles across the corporate, nonprofit and philanthropic sectors. As an advisor, his work is featured in leading outlets such as HBR, Forbes, and Wall Street Journal, and in authoring three books, including the best-seller, Boundary Spanning Leadership. His purpose is to develop leaders, cultures and systems that awaken the best in people to solve problems, innovate and transform.

## Andrew Keyt

Founder and CEO and Advisor of Generation6 Family Enterprise Advisors (*Generation6.com*). He brings over 25 years of professional family business consulting experience and is an internationally known business strategist and succession planning expert. Prior to founding Generation6, Andrew was the President and Founder of Keyt Consulting, a private firm that assists family enterprises with succession and strategic planning, dealing with family conflict and communication, working with adult sibling and cousin teams, and executing emergency management transitions.

### Greg McCann

Founder, Board Member, and Advisor of Generation6 Family Enterprise Advisors (*Generation6.com*). He brings over 30 years of helping individuals who want to work towards success in their careers and lives. Prior to founding Generation6, Greg was the founder of McCann & Associates, a boutique firm that works with family enterprises in the areas of leadership, team building, succession, communication, and conflict resolution with a special emphasis on leadership. Greg has coached leaders, executives, and the rising generation in using both the Leadership Agility and the Myers-Briggs Type Indicator models. He is also the author of two books.

### Jill Shipley

Managing Director and head of Alvarium Tiedemann | AlTi Family Governance and Education Practice (*Tiedemannadvisors.com*). She helps families, family offices, foundations, and family enterprises manage the impact of multigenerational wealth. She brings over 20 years of experience and expertise in family systems, preparing rising generations, communicating about wealth, navigating family enterprise transitions, family and business governance, and strategic philanthropy.

Made in the USA
Las Vegas, NV
12 January 2025

16284856R00109